Over the past twenty years immigration has become one of the most contested issues in western Europe. The arrival of Africans, Asians, eastern Europeans, and others in Italy has reversed earlier trends of emigration. Debate, political activity, and violence have raised questions of rejection and integration, of anti-racism, and the new racism. Studies of these issues commonly focus on political activity and the plight of minorities, but this book breaks new ground in its emphasis on the everyday reactions of Italians to immigration and related issues. Drawing on research carried out in Palermo, Jeffrey Cole considers the role of class, culture, local history, and political economy in the ambivalent responses of Sicilians to immigrants. He places Italian attitudes in a European context, and investigates why anti-immigrant politics are concentrated in the wealthy Italian north.

Cambridge Studies in Social and Cultural Anthropology

107

THE NEW RACISM IN EUROPE

Cambridge Studies in Social and Cultural Anthropology

The monograph series Cambridge Studies in Social and Cultural Anthropology publishes analytical ethnographies, comparative works and contributions to theory. All combine an expert and critical command of ethnography and a sophisticated engagement with current theoretical debates.

A list of books in the series will be found at the end of the volume.

Founding Editors:
Meyer Fortes, Jack Goody, Edmund Leach, Stanley Tambiah

THE NEW RACISM IN EUROPE,

A Sicilian ethnography

JEFFREY COLE
Dowling College, New York

CAMBRIDGE
UNIVERSITY PRESS

PUBLISHED BY THE PRESS SYNDICATE OF THE UNIVERSITY OF CAMBRIDGE
The Pitt Building, Trumpington Street, Cambridge CB2 1RP

CAMBRIDGE UNIVERSITY PRESS
The Edinburgh Building, Cambridge CB2 2RU, United Kingdom
40 West 20th Street, New York, NY 10011-4211, USA
10 Stamford Road, Oakleigh, Melbourne 3166, Australia

First published 1997

Printed in the United Kingdom at the University Press, Cambridge

Typeset in 10/13 pt Monophoto Times   [SE]

A catalogue record for this book is available from the British Library

Library of Congress cataloguing in publication data

Cole, Jeffrey, 1958–
    The new racism in Europe: a Sicilian ethnography / Jeffrey Cole.
        p.   cm – (Cambridge studies in social and cultural
    anthropology: 107)
    Includes bibliographical references and index.
    ISBN 0 521 58493 0 (hardback)
    1. Sicily (Italy) – Ethnic relations.   2. Sicily (Italy) – Race
relations.   3. Sicily (Italy) – Emigration and immigration.
4. Culture conflict – Italy – Sicily.   5. Sicily (Italy) Social
conditions – 1945–   I. Title.   II. Series.
    DG865.7.C65   1997   305.8′009458–dc21   97-4075   CIP

ISBN 0 521 58493 0 hardback

To Sally

Contents

Illustrations

Acknowledgments

In the course of planning, researching, and writing this book I have enjoyed the encouragement and assistance of numerous individuals and institutions both here and abroad.

I consider myself the beneficiary of intellectual stimulus, encouragement, and plain good advice offered freely by teachers, colleagues, and friends. In particular, I would like to thank Jane and Peter Schneider, Glenn Peterson, Leith Mullings, Gary McDonogh, Michael Blim, Eric Wolf, Edward Hansen, David Maynard, D. Chris Leonard, Richard Hara, Malve von Hassell, and Marty Schoenhals. I owe a special debt to Jane Schneider. As a teacher and as adviser to my dissertation at the City University of New York, she initiated me into the craft of ethnography, whose complexities and rewards I am only now beginning to appreciate. Her invitation to a conference on the "Italian Southern Question," sponsored by the Wenner-Gren Foundation, offered me the opportunity to rethink my material.

I have also had the great good fortune to have Jessica Kuper as editor. The publication of this book owes much to her advice and support. I would also like to thank two anonymous readers for the Cambridge University Press, whose comments I found invaluable. Andrew Humphrys deftly copy-edited the manuscript.

I also benefitted from the assistance of many individuals and institutions in Italy. In Rome, Luigi Filadoro of the Commission for Cultural Exchange Between Italy and the United States took pains to ensure that my experience as a Fulbrighter was a memorable one. Giovanna Ghiotto and Augustino Bevilacqua of Progetto Italia-razzismo procured valuable research materials for me. I enjoyed conversations with representatives of Senzaconfine and the Federazione delle Organizzazione e Comunità

Straniere in Italia. In Palermo, representatives of the following organizations generously gave of their time: the Salesian Order, including Oratorio Santa Chiara and the Poliambulatorio in Ballarò; the Centro Immigrazione and the Associazione Siciliana Emigrati e Famiglia of the Chiesa Valdese; Caritàs; the regional office and the Centro La Speranza/Collaboratrici Familiari of the Associazioni Cristiane Lavoratori Italiani; Associazione Professionale Italiana delle Collaboratrici Familiari; Associazione Ellai Illai; Unione Siciliana Emigrati e Famiglie; Centro Informazione Sud-Sud; the Coordinamento Immigrati Sud del Mondo of the Associazione Ricreativa Culturale Italiana; Associazione Regionale degli Immigrati e Famiglie; Confederazione Italiana dei Sindacati Liberi; Confederazione Generale Italiana del Lavoro; Ispettorato Provinciale del Lavoro di Palermo; the Servizio Studi of the Banco di Sicilia; the Tunisian Consulate; and the United States Consulate. I also learned from visits to the Centro Accoglienza Terzomondiale in Alcamo, the Meeting del Mediterraneo in Catania, and Caritàs in Salemi.

While I benefitted from the efforts of many people in Palermo, I found the help of several to be invaluable. Don Cosimo and his staff at the Centro Sociale San Francesco Saverio in Albergheria found accommodation for me and my family, introduced us to the neighborhood, and encouraged and facilitated the study. A better host I cannot imagine. I profited from numerous discussions with Professor Vincenzo Guarrasi, the University of Palermo scholar whose analyses of immigration to Sicily and the political economy of Palermo I have found indispensable. I am indebted to teachers Angela Aiola and Giovanni Callari, who allowed me to administer the questionnaire to their students. Dr. Giovanni Pampanini and Professors Roberto Rovelli, Giuseppe Scidà, and Hassen Slama generously shared their research on immigration. Vincenzo Ognibene let me have the run of the library at the Opera Universitaria, introduced me to Palermitans of all classes, solved all manner of problems, and helped administer the questionnaire to students at the University of Palermo. We sorely miss his companionship and that of his wife, Ida Abbadessa, and their daughter Ardaisia. Like so many Sicilianists before me, I was the grateful recipient of Pasquale Marchese's warm hospitality and profound knowledge of Sicily. We spent many memorable days with him, his son Vincenzo, and Elena Paparcone at *il mulino*. Whenever we think of Sicily our thoughts turn to the old mill and to Pasquale's wisdom. Our affection for Sicily grew at the table of Mary Taylor Simeti and Antonio Simeti, whose daughter Natalia took good care of our son Sammy. Fara Mejia was a boon companion to my wife and afforded me an insider's view of an immigrant's life. Doug Barnes of the United States Information Agency and Mary Benton shared their passion for Sicily with us and gave us all kinds of practical help. We also enjoyed the company of Sal Cucchiari, Kate Loring, Rosario Lentini, Fausta Ferruzza, Giovanna Albegiani, Liana Castelli, and Fabrizio Mangione. Finally, this study would not have been possible without the patience and hospitality of Palermitans too numerous to name. I thank the respondents in the school and neighborhood samples, who shall remain anonymous, as well as the immigrants with whom I spoke. I am especially indebted to the people of Albergheria who showed me and my family such warm hospitality and generosity.

Throughout the project I have drawn encouragement and affection from my family. My parents, Rosemary and E. Larry Cole, have offered unstinting support, as has my father-in-law, Charles F. Booth. Jocelyn and Sam make life a delight and an adventure. I reserve my greatest thanks for my wife, Sally Starbuck Booth. My keenest critic and most ardent supporter, she helped me through all aspects of the research. She introduced me to Sicily and taught me the techniques of research during her own fieldwork there in 1988. It was she who first noted the the paradox of immigration to Sicily and urged me to develop it as a dissertation topic. To Sally, the love of my life, I dedicate this work.

I received financial support for doctoral research in the form of a Dissertation Award from the Harry Frank Guggenheim Foundation, a Grant for Improving Doctoral Research from the National Science Foundation (number BNS-9012923), a Fulbright Award for Graduate Study, and a Grant-in-Aid of Research from Sigma Xi. A Richard Carley Hunt Memorial Postdoctoral Fellowship from the Wenner-Gren Foundation allowed me to devote a summer to revising the dissertation into a book. Dowling College has generously supported my endeavors. I presented the results of this research at Dowling's Mediterranean Conference in 1995 and 1996; I am grateful to the conference organizer, Norman Holub, for giving me the opportunity to participate. Released time from Dowling enabled me to complete revisions to this manuscript in a timely manner. I gratefully acknowledge these sources of funding and institutional support.

I would also like to thank *Critique of Anthropology*. Parts of chapter 2 appeared in "Working-Class Reactions to the New Immigration in Palermo (Italy)," *Critique of Anthropology* 16(2): 199–220.

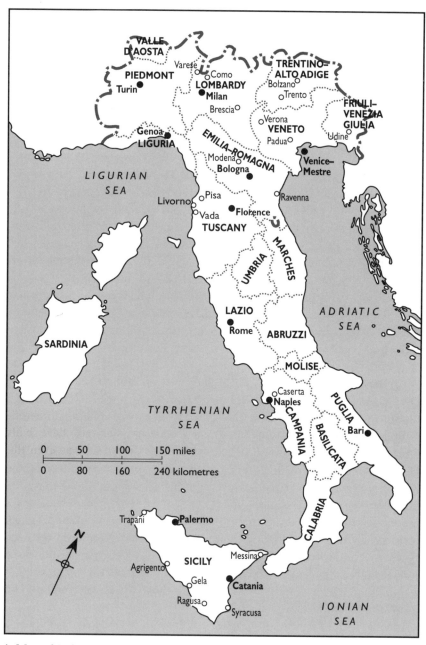

1. Map of Italy

1

Introduction

Questions

Italy, long a country of emigration, has become a country of immigration in the past two decades with the arrival of nearly one million Africans, Asians, and others. This transformation has surprised politicians and citizens, who had come to regard emigration as part of Italian life. This change is particularly striking in the southern region of Sicily. For most of the last 100 years, oppression and poverty have generated waves of emigration from Sicily, first overseas and later, in the postwar period, to the Italian north and to western Europe. For much of this century, one out of every eight Italian emigrants was a Sicilian; and in the decade 1951–61 alone nearly 400,000 Sicilians left home (Renda 1989: 122–3; 18). From Brooklyn to Toronto, from Milan to Frankfurt, Sicilians have built bridges, dug tunnels, and constructed office buildings; and, as even the casual tourist knows, they have brought their shops, bakeries, and restaurants to far-flung Little Italies.

The 1970s witnessed a profound change in migratory patterns as many Sicilians returned and newcomers arrived.[1] Among the first to arrive were Tunisians, who toiled in the fields, vineyards, and fisheries. Cape Verdian, Mauritian, and Filipino women served as domestics in homes of the urban rich. In the course of the 1980s some two dozen other nationalities, mostly from Africa and Asia, joined them, swelling the ranks of immigrants to about 15,000 in Palermo alone (*Giornale di Sicilia*, 6 September 1990). By the end of 1990, 62,000 foreigners held residence permits issued in Sicily, making it the country's third-largest immigrant population behind the regions of Lazio and Lombardy (Montanari and Cortese 1993: 287). Sicily's total foreign population, including significant numbers of unregistered immigrants, may have exceeded 100,000 (ISTAT 1990a: 73–5).

In an effort to fathom the contours of this new immigration, and especially how Sicilians have responded to it, I conducted anthropological research in Palermo. For most of 1990 I lived in a poor neighborhood in the decrepit old center, gathering data through participant-observation, discussion, interviews, and questionnaire responses. I aimed to determine the form, extent, and political potential of racist and other views towards immigrants held by the working classes. Later, I expanded my interest to include the responses of the bourgeoisie as well as those of the churches, unions, and associations concerned with immigration issues. I was interested in whether and how immigrant employment posed a threat – or was thought to pose one – to Sicilian workers. In addition to the obvious issue of competition, I sought answers to questions involving key features of Sicilian history and culture. What role does the emigrant experience play in Sicilian evaluations of immigrants? Do Sicilians see Africans and Asians as similar to themselves or as too different to become contributors to Italian society? Is this difference described in racial or cultural terms? How does the widespread anti-southernism within Italy – some northerners deride southerners as "Africans" – complicate Sicilian understandings of physical and cultural difference. Finally, why are anti-immigrant politics and skinhead and neo-nazi attacks on foreigners concentrated in the rich north but absent in the poor south?

A focus on everyday European responses to immigrants distinguishes this study from most current research on race and racism. Some observers have shown that while foreign workers made significant contributions to postwar economic growth, they continue to experience discrimination and institutionalized disadvantage (Castles 1984; Castles and Kosack 1985; Essed 1991). Others have argued that anti-immigrant political movements such as Jean-Marie Le Pen's National Front (FN – Front National) in France constitute a "new racism" in which immigrants are portrayed as dangerous and threatening (Balibar 1991a, 1991b; Barker 1981; Taguieff 1989, 1990). Productive as these perspectives are, scholars have pursued them to the neglect of the important issue of how Europeans, on an everyday level, think about and treat immigrants, and the attendant ideologies of difference. I suggest that what is needed to complement research on inequality and political discourse is an ethnography that investigates how class and local history shape the ways people do and do not give expression to the entangled issues of immigration, race, and culture.

This book seeks to contribute to such an ethnographic enterprise. Two main concerns orient this account. The first examines the ways class and culture shape Palermitans' views of immigrants. I take up working-class and bourgeois responses to immigrants, respectively, in chapters 2 and 3. The goal here is to relate the material experience and aspirations of Palermitans to their views on immigration and race, and to identify tendencies and contradictions. The second concern, the politicization of immigration, is addressed in chapter 4, where I discuss the most prominent churches, unions, and associations that formulate and disseminate paradigms to guide interpretation and action with regard to immigration. Like many bourgeois Palermitans, representatives of these institutions and associations urge Sicilians to treat immigrants with a tolerance born of the memory of Sicilian emigration experience. Chapter 4 also contrasts the intense politicization of immigration and race in the north with the tepid response in the south, and relates the divergence to regional differences in economy and politics.

The remainder of this introductory chapter establishes the context of study, first describing immigration to Italy and Italian reactions to it, then considering what studies of trends elsewhere in western Europe can say about the question of the treatment and reception of immigrants in Sicily. I close with a description of the site, methods, and findings of the research.

Immigration to Italy
The transformation of Italy into a country of immigration reflects a general shift in postwar European migratory patterns. Before most western European countries imposed restrictions on immigration in 1973–4, governments and businesses in most industrial areas had actively recruited mostly young men from colonies and former colonies or, lacking these, from the northern rim of the Mediterranean basin, deploying them on a temporary basis in construction, industry, and low-level services in urban areas (Berger and Mohr 1975; Bohning 1984; Castles and Kosack 1985; Miles and Satzewich 1990; Therborn 1987). In German-speaking countries, these workers were euphemistically called *gastarbeiter* or "guestworkers." So great was the demand for labor power in the context of the postwar boom that the number of foreign workers in Belgium, France, West Germany, Britain, the Netherlands, Sweden, and Switzerland rose from six million in 1960 to thirteen million in 1970 (Castles and Kosack 1985: 490).

The ongoing "new immigration," by contrast, is characterized by more permanent immigrant communities of increasingly non-European origins. By 1980, approximately 40 percent of the estimated sixteen million immigrants in western Europe hailed from non-European countries (Castles and Kosack 1985: 490–2). The new population is, moreover, unsolicited and often unregulated or undocumented (Castles 1984; King 1993a; Melotti 1989). Newcomers often perform menial jobs in the informal sector, reflecting an increasingly segmented labor market in which demand for temporary, unprotected, and low-wage labor proliferates in poor as well as rich areas (Calvanese and Pugliese 1988; Guarrasi 1982a; Pugliese 1993). Geographically more dispersed than the earlier immigration, the new immigration concerns not only the traditional countries of immigration such as France and Switzerland but also former sender countries such as Greece, Spain, and, most prominently, Italy.

Immigration to Italy began in significant numbers in the 1970s and grew steadily throughout the 1980s in the context of economic growth and the near absence of immigration controls (Calvanese and Pugliese 1988; Guarrasi 1982a; Montanari and Cortese 1993). During the period 1986–90, Italy replaced West Germany as Europe's largest recipient of mass immigration (King 1993b: 283). By 1990's end, 781,000 foreigners possessed residence permits in Italy, a figure that would rise to 896,767 the following year (Monticelli 1992: 64). Although present throughout the country, foreigners are concentrated in urban areas in the center and north. Regions with the largest foreign populations (in 1990) include: Lazio (197,000 or 25.2 percent), Lombardy (117,000 or 15 percent), Sicily (62,000 or 7.9 percent), Tuscany (61,000 or 7.8 percent), and Veneto (50,000 or 6.4 percent) (Montanari and Cortese 1993: 286).

Typical of current European trends, the composition of the foreigner workforce in Italy is varied. Newcomers hail from dozens of countries and from all corners of the globe; citizens of no single country account for more than 10 percent of the total foreign population. Although politicians and many observers tend to equate immigrants with the Third World, registered foreigners also include citizens of other European Union (EU) member states, citizens of non-EU industrialized nations such as the United States, descendants of Italian emigrants holding foreign passports, and non-Italian members of religious orders. In broad strokes, almost a quarter (24.5 percent or 288,000) of the 781,000 documented foreigners in Italy come from advanced capitalist countries in the EU and elsewhere. The majority (63 percent or 493,000) derive from so-called "less developed countries" (LDCs) in Africa, Asia, Latin America, and eastern Europe, with the largest numbers coming from Morocco, Tunisia, the Philippines, former Yugoslavia, Senegal, Egypt, China, Poland, and Iran (Montanari and Cortese 1993: 286). Estimates of illegally present or undocumented foreigners, most of whom are thought to come from poor countries, range from 100,000 (Monticelli 1992) to 420,000 (Montanari and Cortese 1993: 290).

This account is concerned with the condition and reception of foreigners from these less developed countries. These newcomers to Italy are typically young, single, and recently arrived in Italy; men outnumber women slightly; and Christians outnumber Muslims two to one (CENSIS 1990a; CNEL 1990). The employment of foreigners varies by sex, nationality, region, and over time, but a general pattern is evident (CENSIS 1990a; Cocchi 1989; CNEL 1990; King 1993b; Macioti and Pugliese 1991; Pugliese 1989; Raffaele 1992; Venturini 1989). They do the most menial, low-paying, and hazardous jobs, and commonly accept undocumented or off-the-books employment, which in Italian is called *lavoro nero,* or "black work," and does not refer to skin color.[2]

For immigrants, work in the tertiary sector predominates, followed by work in the primary sector, and, less commonly, in the secondary sector. Domestic work is the most stable, most often documented, and best paying of service-sector jobs; this is typically found in cities and often involves living with the employer. These servants are called *colf,* the acronym for the euphemistic term, *collaboratrice familiare* or "family helper." Christian women from the Philippines, Cape Verde, and other countries tend to work as *colf,* although some Italians returning from Somalia and Ethiopia in recent decades have brought servants back with them. All groups, but especially North Africans and Middle Easterners, work in low-level positions of varying stability in service jobs, in restoration work, in restaurants, bars, hotels, and gas stations. Many Moroccans and Senegalese ply the unstable trade of the itinerant street vendor, known as *vu cumprà,*[3] selling Africana and inexpensive seasonal objects from seashore to city throughout the country. Because the street vendors work in public and typically lack required licenses, police monitor their activities and occasionally confiscate their stock (Khouma 1990). Employment in the primary sector is particularly important in the south. Mostly North and sub-Saharan Africans find unsteady work and low pay as agricultural day laborers. An exception to the unsteady work in this sector is found in Mazara del Vallo in Sicily, where many in the large (5,000-strong) Tunisian community work in the fishing industry. Finally, some immigrants find fairly stable work in construction and manufacturing in the north of Italy.

Italian reactions
Italian debate on immigration dates from the late 1980s, when it became clear that Italy lacked an administrative and even cultural framework for the ever-increasing influx of foreigners. By 1988, the topic had captured

national attention. The media, from serious newspapers to weekly magazines to television variety shows, reported attacks on and discrimination against foreigners, and surveyed Italian attitudes to foreigners. Intellectuals worried over the potential for Le Pen-like xenophobia in Italy and called for tolerance of diversity. An increasing volume of social-science research on immigration issues also began to be published (e.g., Balbo 1990; Bassetti 1990; Cocchi 1989; Calvanese and Pugliese 1988; Caritàs Diocesana 1985; Gallini 1989; Giardesco 1988; Manconi 1990; SIARES 1988). As churches established programs to aid immigrants, unions and associations sponsored "anti-racist" events such as conferences, rallies, and concerts. In Rome, scholars and parliamentarians drew on the example of "SOS Racisme," an anti-racist organization associated with immigrant and French youth in France, to found "Progetto Italia-razzismo" (Balbo and Manconi 1990). Immigrants themselves formed associations, both along lines of nationality and across them, as in the case of the Federazione delle Organizzazioni e Comunità Straniere in Italia (FOCSI–Federation of Foreign Organizations and Communities in Italy). They also found representation in some Italian associations. The Associazione Ricreativa Culturale Italiana (Italian Recreational and Cultural Association), for example, formed an office devoted to immigration matters and staffed by immigrants (Coordinamento Immigrati Sud del Mondo, or ARCI–CISM). This concern peaked in 1990, after decree #416 became Law #39 in January, and after the six-month registration period for foreigners closed in June.

Law #39, also known as the "Martelli law" after its sponsor, the Socialist Claudio Martelli,[4] concerns the entry, residence, and employment of refugees, foreign students, and foreign workers. The law allows for the expulsion of foreigners who are illegally present or who commit crimes. Its enactment also temporarily closed the border by prohibiting entry to all but refugees, family members of registered immigrants, and those employees expressly summoned by employers (see Forti (1990), Nascimbene (1990), and Zanchetta (1991) for full descriptions of the law and its implementation). For immigrants present in Italy before the end of 1989, the law provides the opportunity to *regolarizzarsi*, or legalize their status, with residence and work permits of two years' duration, the right to enroll at public employment offices, and various social services. The Martelli law, Italy's first comprehensive legislation regulating resident foreigners, brought Italy into conformity with the laws of other EU member states in anticipation of the 1992 opening of internal borders. The law facilitates the legal absorption of immigrants at the same time as it closes borders

2. Benetton ad, central business district, Palermo. This is an example of Benetton's campaign for racial tolerance.

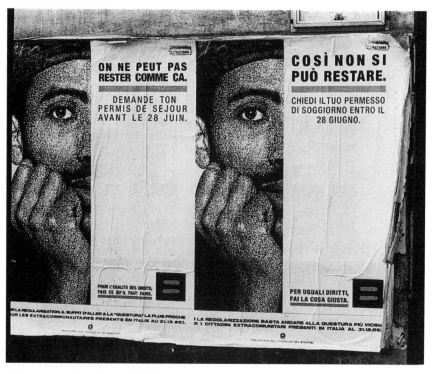

3. Poster, immigration legislation. The poster appeared in cities throughout Italy and in a number of languages. It exhorts the immigrant to register under Law #39, and reads, "You Can't Go On Like This. Request Your Residency Permit by 28 June. For Equal Rights, Do the Right Thing."

until further laborers are deemed necessary. In effect, it enables the state to manage foreign labor as a resource.[5]

In retrospect, the Martelli law served as a turning point in Italian reactions to immigration. The tone of the early debate was mostly set by left-of-center intellectuals and activists, as well as a few politicians, and their tone was essentially positive. Rare were warnings such as that issued by the well-known economics professor Paolo Sylos Labini (1988: 147), that North Africans "bring with them problems of terrorism and public order." Rather, many activists set out to aid immigrants and to publicize their cause. They called for responsible legislation to regulate immigration, and established structures to assist immigrants with jobs, housing, health care, and permits. In general, activists regarded immigrants as more a resource than a problem, seeing in them the potential for a new and pluralistic Italy.

A concern with race also figured prominently in the activists' ideas (Pugliese 1991). They asked: who are these "immigrants of color" (*immigrati di colore*) and "blacks" (*neri*), and how do Italians treat them? The title of an early book by the noted journalist Giorgio Bocca (1988) posed the lightning-rod question – *Are Italians Racist?* The question preoccupied many because since World War II Italians had learned to condemn as inhumane any form of *razzismo* ("racism"). Seldom defined, this term is used to mean hostility, violence, or intolerance directed against culturally and physically different populations.

Two kinds of answers emerged. Not a few assumed that Italians were in fact "immune to racism." As Dacia Maraini (1990) recalls:

I always remember having heard, from my childhood on, that Italians "by nature are immune to racism." "Italy was Fascist," it was said, "out of ignorance, out of conformism, out of fear, but it was never blinded by racist hate." "How many Italians in Africa," someone added, "paired off with black girls, and even had children."[6]

Others sought to puncture what they regarded as a complacent myth of "good" or tolerant Italians (*italiani, brava gente*). They condemned the "racist" exploitation of foreign workers, and cited a disturbing number of attacks on foreigners in addition to opinion surveys revealing unanticipated hostility towards foreigners (e.g., Comunità di Sant'Egidio 1989, cited in Bassetti 1990: 44). Yet neither was this view free from the optimism of Italian society's ideals of tolerance and diversity. The prominent sociologist, Franco Ferrarotti (1989), for example, entitled his 1988 book *Beyond Racism: Towards a Multicultural and Multiracial Society.*[7]

Idealism and a certain *naïveté* distinguish the early debate. Perhaps the role of the partisans in the liberation of northern Italy from the Italian Fascists and the Nazis at the end of World War II has a bearing on this tendency. The importance of the Communists[8] in the liberation movement and in postwar politics, particularly in the "Red Belt" of central Italy, may explain the prominence of ideologies of racial equality and the lack of Italian guilt over the Jews and gypsies surrendered to the Germans in the war. Laura Balbo, co-founder of Italia-razzismo and a Member of Parliament, characterizes much of the early debate as "facile anti-racism." These anti-racists simply declare themselves for what is good ("anti-racism") and against what is bad ("racism," "all the racisms") without defining or justifying their terms; or they romantically and uncritically embrace the descriptive term "pluralism" as an ideal (Balbo 1989, 1990). Enrico Pugliese (1991) has drily observed that the supposed lapses of the "facile" opponents of racism hardly constitute a danger to immigrants or to the emerging debate when immigrants are daily subject to exploitation and violence. At any rate, a high idealism does indeed typify much Italian debate. Up until the passage of the "Martelli law" and the subsequent closing of the borders, for example, many progressives dismissed as folly even the notion of officially closing the borders because the demographic, economic, and political forces driving immigration were clearly too compelling for regulation. (According to Balbo, institutions such as churches, unions, and associations embarked on more pragmatic initiatives from 1989 even as they continued to voice a naïve optimism. Several of these were important in bringing about legislative change.)

Bitter debate over the Martelli decree did much to darken the mood of Italian debate on immigration. As anticipated, the neo-fascist Italian Social Movement (MSI – Movimento Sociale Italiano; now the National Alliance) and the Lombard League (LL – Lega Lombarda; now the Northern League[9]) objected to the legislation. In their view, immigrants take jobs away from deserving Italians, provoke an understandable if lamentable defensive reaction among them, and present insurmountable problems of cultural difference. More significant were objections to the law made by the Republican Party (PRI – Partito Repubblicano Italiano), a small but influential member of numerous postwar coalition governments. As an outspoken opponent of the decree, the PRI's respected leader, Giorgio La Malfa, made anti-immigrant views acceptable to many. As the decree was being passed into law merchants in Florence organized a march that was in effect a thinly veiled claim that immigrants had brought drugs and disorder to that historic city. Several days later in the same streets, a gang of masked young men beat immigrants under cover of Carnival celebrations. Opponents of the law supported the merchants' protest, which would become a model for similar protests elsewhere in the north. Though they condemned the Carnival assault as "racist," they insinuated that more violence would result from continued immigration, which they implied would result with the implementation of the Martelli law.

Once the law was passed, its opponents successfully enacted a provision that closed the borders until further consideration. Despite its prominence in the immigration debate, the PRI failed to achieve electoral gains. More successful were the MSI and LL, who called for the repeal of the law, and mobilized working people against the plans of various city governments to provide temporary facilities for immigrants. The government's commitment to closed borders, strikingly exemplified by the 1991 expulsion of Albanian refugees, found reflection in opinion polls showing increasing intolerance (Bonifazi 1992) and in a series of violent attacks on foreigners.

European perspectives

Research on anti-immigrant trends elsewhere in western Europe has a bearing on the study of Italian reactions. For instance, studies show the continued marginalization of immigrants, even as their composition and distribution has changed under the new immigration. By every socio-economic indicator their lives remain more difficult than those of the indigenous working class (Castles and Kosack 1985; Skellington 1992). In terms of class, most constitute what Stephen Castles and Godula Kosack call lower "strata" of the working class. Relegated for the most part to menial jobs and concentrated in depressed urban areas, these populations have little chance of upward mobility and bear the stigma of minority status. Other researchers have probed the ways political action and rhetoric, news reporting, and popular culture conspire to create an image of immigrants as problematic for Europe (e.g., Balibar 1991a, 1991b, 1991c; Castles 1984; CCCS 1982; Donald and Rattansi 1992; Essed 1991; Gilroy 1987; Grimm and Hermand 1986; Hartmann and Husband 1974; Husband 1987a; McDonogh 1992; Silverman 1991; Solomos 1989; Van Dijk 1988, 1991; Wrench and Solomos 1993). Resultant essentialist ideologies portray immigrants as different and threatening, and as non-contributors who cannot or will not fit in. In 1970s England, for example, the official position asserted that the arrival of West Indians and Asians had created a problem called "race relations" (Miles 1982). As Stuart Hall has noted, such a stance betrays a "profound historical forgetfulness" of the role of British colonialism in the creation of racial inequality and categories.

While foreign workers were generally tolerated as necessary during the economic expansion of the 1950s and 1960s, they became seen as problems as economic downturn, restructuring, and political crisis gripped western Europe from the mid-1970s. By the late 1980s, violence and political attacks were mounted by far-right groups on refugees, Jews and gypsies, and especially immigrants (European Parliament 1991). According to the Runnymeade Trust, 6,459 racially motivated incidents occurred in England and Wales in 1990 (Skellington 1992: 63). In recently reunited Germany, neo-nazi groups have attacked African, Asian, and eastern European refugees, as well as Jews and Turks; sixteen people died in 2,285 attacks in 1992 (*New York Times,* 2 December 1992; 17 January 1993). Jean-Marie Le Pen's National Front (FN) is perhaps the best known of over a dozen populist-nationalist and neo-fascist parties that denounce these targeted peoples as threats to European cultural integrity, economic viability, and social peace (Husbands 1992). The FN claims that "foreigners," whether they be French citizens and resident for generations or recently arrived, are France's greatest problem. In response to the electoral success of Le Pen and others, mainstream parties throughout Europe have adopted anti-immigrant policies; examples include, in France, the Union of French Democracy (UDF) and Rally for the Republic (RPR), and the German Christian Social Union (CSU) and Social Democratic Party (SPD).

A number of scholars argue that such ideologies constitute a novel form of racism, whether "new racism" (Barker 1981), "neo-racism" (Balibar 1991a), or "differentialist racism" (Taguieff 1989, 1990). In their view, Le Pen and others treat targeted populations (including immigrants) as naturally occurring groups whose fundamental difference and inferiority furnish sufficient reason for the curtailment of their opportunities in Europe if not outright repatriation. Faced with the official repudiation of racism, the memory of Nazism and Fascism, and a vocal "anti-racist" lobby, the ideologues of intolerance have discarded the rhetoric of race for that of culture and nation. While such ideologies are new to the extent that they denigrate culture and nationality rather than skin color, they reiterate the former colonialist vision of humanity as made up of bounded, natural, and unequal peoples. Race, then, refers not to a monolithic concept but to a process (called "racialization" by some) by which socially significant populations are represented as naturally constituted populations of unequal merit. As a social product, racial ideologies vary in specific content, mode of expression, and relation to the patterns of inequality to which they are linked (Balibar 1991b, 1991d; Gallissot 1989; Guillaumin 1995; Husband 1987b, 1987c; Miles 1989; Rattansi 1992; Reeves 1983; Wieviorka 1992).

The new ideologies often center on the role of the state because it regulates immigration, defines citizenship and rights, administers services, oversees the economy, and sanctifies national culture. As a result, nationalism and race have become increasingly entangled in contemporary Europe. Le Pen, for example, would preserve the integrity of France by instituting a state-regulated system of "national preference", which would halt immigration, allow for repatriation, reserve jobs for nationals, and create legal distinctions between "real" French and "foreigners" (Taguieff 1989: 47–8). It is significant that in this interpretation the category of "foreigner" does not include the descendants of the numerous Italian, Belgian, and Spanish immigrants who, in the 1880s and again in the 1930s, were previously the targets of xenophobic violence and stereotyping in France (Noiriel 1988; Schor 1985). Once thought incapable of assimilation, these former immigrants are now considered of "French stock" (*français de souche*). Instead, Le Pen focuses his attack on residents from France's former colonies and possessions, especially in North Africa, including many with French citizenship. In sum, the term "new racism" encompasses a trend in contemporary European politics, but the ideologies themselves vary in content, intensity, and popular support, as do the anti-racist movements that contest them.

The contradictory actions of European states within the context of late capitalism provide a context for the problematization of immigration (Miles 1993: 200–7; see also Balibar 1991b). In response to the general perception that immigration is detrimental to receiving societies, European states have sought to incorporate resident foreigners through programs of integration and to restrict further ingress. Yet governments have found themselves unable and unwilling to stop population movements for a number of reasons, including laws on family reunification and political asylum, the posting of government employees, and the movement of professionals from within and outside the EU. Given this structural contradiction, governments have adopted the "ideological solution" of defining immigration narrowly as Third World in origin and problematic in nature. This move keeps out of the debate (as of the 1980s) some five million EU government employees and retirees, and professional migrants from other industrialized countries, such as the United States.

In the current context the very use and meaning of terms like "foreigner," "immigrants," "racism," and "European" are thus objects of political struggle. At issue is the political redefinition of Europe, the allocation of resources among citizens and resident foreigners, and the relationship of an integrated Europe with the rest of the world. The populations somehow held responsible for European dilemmas are quite diverse and include recent immigrants and refugees, Jews and gypsies, and established immigrant communities. The relationship of these populations with their European countries of residence is also complex: some come from former colonies and possess European passports, others come from the Third World or the former Eastern Bloc, while Jews possess both European citizenship and a strong supranational identity. While acknowledging that significant numbers of resident foreigners from rich countries fall outside of this definition, in this account I shall use "immigrant" and occasionally "foreigner" and the "Other" as shorthand for these diverse and embattled peoples. The question of racism is indissolubly linked to immigration in postwar, postcolonial Europe; and, in the case of Italy, most of the people in question are in fact immigrants.

The Italian context revisited

The perspectives outlined so far shed much light on the presence of immigrants in Italy. Three phenomena in particular – the labor market, politics, and popular culture – relegate immigrants to the margins of Italian society and problematize them as physically and culturally different from Italians.

Economic subordination plays an important role in the exploitation and marking of immigrants. While a number of foreigners have high-school and university educations, few possess much capital. Precarious legal status is also an important reason why so many find themselves languishing in low-paying and temporary jobs. The creation of a sizable pool of vulnerable foreign-born workers derives from the actions of the Italian state in the context of impressive economic growth (Guarrasi 1982a; Sciortino 1988, 1991; Sestino 1989). From the decision to close the borders in 1982 to the passage of Law #39 in 1990, the state permitted record numbers of entries while making meager efforts to offer immigrants the possibility of legal status and the protections that theoretically affords. Until 1990 the status of the majority of immigrants was illegal or semi-legal at best. The inconsistent and inadequate processing of permits under amnesty programs in 1986 and 1988 (offered through Laws #941 and #81 respectively) allowed rather few immigrants to obtain fully legal status. The need to secure proof of what amounted to undocumented employment from employers knowingly breaking the law also prevented many immigrants from taking advantage of the law's provisions. In the process "black work," which had no previous racial connotation, is becoming associated with the work of "blacks." In this way economic marginalization underwrites an overarching definition of immigrants as different and lesser than Italians.

In sum, government inaction in the 1980s shaped immigration into what Giovanna Campani (1993: 511–12) has called a prolonged "social emergency" in which foreigners were left vulnerable on the labor market, bereft of any social infrastructure, and separated from the organizations and protections afforded many working Italians. Reinforcing the sense of crisis was a housing crisis in the north, where high rents, housing shortages, and discrimination have reduced many foreigners to homeless squatters and transients (Cuffaro 1990a, 1990b). It is no accident that the statistically insignificant *vu cumprà* figured prominently in Italian images of immigrants in the late 1980s. Transient and poor, dependent on transactions with Italians but independent and unknown to any community, these itinerant peddlers embody the marginal Other and recall the poverty and hopelessness of the Third World.

The Martelli law altered, to some extent, the relationship of immigrants with the labor market. Within six months, over 230,000 foreigners had legalized their status, more than double that during the earlier amnesties (*Giornale di Sicilia,* 30 October 1990). There was an immediate increase in demand for permit-holding foreigners in northern industry, which accelerated the ongoing movement of immigrants from the south to the north, from the inevitability of black work to the possibility of legal pay and benefits. Yet this new-found status, as beneficial as it is, does not guarantee legal employment. Like not a few Italians, many immigrants will continue to accept the terms of black work, whether out of necessity or out of the desire for tax-free income. This holds especially true in the south, where employers in agriculture rarely document their mostly seasonal workers.

The economic subordination of foreign workers builds on and interacts with ideologies of difference, but does not in itself create them. In Italy, the problematization of immigrants is in large measure the result of political activity, both pro- and anti-immigrant, that addresses from different perspectives the "social emergency." Mostly, leftist proponents of immigrant rights dominated the early debate, working to secure decent conditions for foreigners. This practical activity also promoted the conceptual meshing of race and immigration. Activists denounced the economic exploitation of immigrants and violence against them as expressions of *razzismo.* Common terms describing foreigners as "blacks" and "immigrants of color" invoked the political language of race, recalling by association the horrors of racial oppression in South Africa and the United States. At the same time they extolled the project of a multi-racial Italy in which individuals would be integrated irrespective of physical appearance. By giving salience to immigration as a racial phenomenon, the Italian cultural elite tapped the powerful contemporary condemnation of racism to serve the rhetorical defense of immigrants. As a result, discussions on topics from the exploitation of foreigners to their legal status to their political fate turned frequently to the question of *razzismo.*

While this self-styled "anti-racist" activity contributed in an unexpected way to the problematization of immigrants, vociferous anti-immigrant mobilizations by the center-right PRI, MSI, and LL strove to vilify foreigners. Lacking a mass base and clinging to an ideological commitment to liberalism, the small PRI was unable to make significant gains to its political capital out of its objections to the Martelli law. More efficient and bold in their approach to the issue, the MSI and the LL in particular took their concerns to the people, denouncing the "africanization" of cities and fomenting opposition to government plans to house immigrants. The Lombard League has been described as a "populist-nationalist" party because its main concerns are regional autonomy (at least, initially) and government corruption and inefficiency (Poche 1991–2; Woods 1992). League spokesmen have nevertheless repeatedly defined southern Italians and immigrants as troublesome, accusing southerners of draining resources from the north by virtue of their alleged control of the central state, and attacking immigrants for being a financial burden and too culturally distant to be assimilated into Italian life. Like the new racists elsewhere, League leaders confront the arguments of anti-racism in a subtle way: they repudiate overt racist violence and shun racial terminology, while phrasing implacable opposition to foreigners in terms of seemingly acceptable themes such as the necessity of law and order and the defense of local economic interests. But, in effect, this stance portrays immigrants as intrinsically problematic, as too different to merit integration into civil society or to justify government intervention.

In addition to the segmented labor market and political mobilization, the problematization of immigrants in Italy owes much to widespread western views of non-westerners. In broad ideological terms, the subjects of western colonialism were constituted dialectically as others whose biological inferiority and proximity to nature contrasted unfavorably to the superior stock and civilization of Europeans (Miles 1989; Stocking 1968). Ideologies of nationalism intersected with racist ideologies as European nation-states, competing with each other for overseas and European territories, fashioned themselves as natural entities whose unique cultural and biological legacies underwrote claims to grandeur (Anderson 1983; Balibar 1991d; Barzun 1967; Poliakov 1974). The Fascist period in Italy represents a critical moment in the making of Italian nationalist ideology in this regard. Mussolini, for example, favorably compared the Aryan stock of the Italians and Germans with those of diverse "inferior races," including the Romanians, Greeks, "Levantines," and the incorrigible British. Racist notions found codification in the racial laws of 1938, which classified as inferior and menacing both the Jews in Italy and the Arabs and Ethiopians, whose countries Mussolini had invaded (Mack Smith 1982).[10]

Despite the official and widespread postwar condemnation of fascism and racism, race continues to be considered an obvious and appropriate descriptive category for the inhabitants of the former colonial world. In Italy, as elsewhere in Europe, discourse on race remains situated in relations of global inequality, as culturally and physically marked populations have passed from the former political powerlessness of colonialism to the contemporary economic powerlessness of dependency and debt. Inequality is explained ideologically as the opposition between "universalistic and progressive" cultures and "irredeemably particularistic and primitive" ones (Balibar 1991a). This dichotomizing representation is, however, a flexible form of hierarchy, which simultaneously unifies and differentiates: the poor Tunisian is clearly an "Arab," whose presence in the west is troublesome, while the Tunisian capitalist finds acceptance in the democracy of money (Balibar 1991c).

An incident described by Bocca (1988) exemplifies this process in Italy. An American bank was to open a branch in Naples and it was rumored that jobs would be allotted to "blacks." Local residents strenuously objected to what they portrayed as the injustice of being passed over for undeserving newcomers. Protests ceased, however, when it was learned that the blacks in question were American. They clearly deserved these positions by virtue of their association with big business from the dominant country in the global economy.

While left-of-center debate on immigration in Italy tends to be moralistic,[11] the complexity and ambivalence of Western attitudes to race finds significant, ongoing expression in popular culture. On this fertile ideological terrain the Western self is contrasted dialectically to the racial Other, which becomes the object of fascination and horror, eroticism and derision. Several recent studies of Italian popular images have suggested that movies, advertisements, travel brochures, arcade games, and so-called "porno-comics" (*pornofumetti*) represent the racial (or ethnic) Other as different from (white) Italians by nature and culture. Clara Gallini's (1989) examination of popular images of Arabs reveals a changing stereotype, evoked by images of sand, palm trees, and camels, whose core remains defined by despotism, sexual perversity, extreme gender inequality, and fanatical Islam. This essentializing Orientalism (Said 1978) is reproduced within a political context. Originating during the period of conflict between Europe and the Ottoman Turks, revived by Fascist propaganda, the stereotype of the Arab now speaks to current Middle Eastern conflict. Recent American news media and movies in particular, portray Arabs as Islamic fanatics and terrorists. Pier Paolo Leschiutta (1989) finds similar images among schoolchildren, university students, and adults in Rome and Naples.

These findings are paralleled by the double representation of blacks in Italy as both African savage and glamorous American black sports or entertainment star. According to Alessandro Portelli (1989), the dichotomized images of blacks perpetuate racial stereotypes in different ways. The image of the savage is used ironically by intellectuals, who claim thereby to reject racist stereotypes; but the continued use of the image perpetuates the idea of blacks as utterly different. The second, more positive, image comes from youth culture, but it too lays emphasis on bodily prowess and therefore on "natural" difference. In my research, I found that Sicilians of all classes also divide their representations of black Americans between the dangerous ghetto and the glamorous sports celebrity, supporting Portelli's claim that the Italian image of blacks is profoundly ambivalent and essentializing. Even southern Italian identification with the exploitation and anger of blacks ultimately shores up the racial denigration it protests: "Rather than identifying with the explorer in the pot we identify with the negroes who dance around him, ready to eat him; but we risk keeping the representation of the scene permanently intact"[12] (Portelli 1989: 97).

Of the perspectives reviewed above, political–economic analyses demonstrate the role of foreign workers in a changing labor market and relate the movement of people to the globalization of capital. Analyses of politics and popular culture reveal the power and adaptability of essentialist ideologies that stigmatize populations excluded from power and so facilitate their exploitation. The state figures in the politicization of these issues. Both anti-"foreigner" and "anti-racist" movements invoke the state and national culture in their divergent aims of cultural purity and diversity. The insecurity of the current political and economic resorting of Europe will encourage the continued entanglement of race and nation.

These perspectives provide a useful background to this study of Sicilian reactions to recent immigration; but they do not go far enough, since they leave largely unexplored the question of how Europeans interact with and view immigrants.[13] The silence on everyday reactions is all the more vexing because commentators acknowledge that ideologies and actions vary significantly by class, and also by region and sex (Husband 1987b; Miles 1989; Van Dijk 1987). In the burgeoning literature on immigration to Italy, for example, the bulk of research concerns policy and the causes and conditions of immigration (e.g., CENSIS 1990a, 1990b; CNEL 1990; Cocchi 1989; Macioti and Pugliese 1991). Italian researchers have yet seriously to consider subtle forms of racism and discrimination (Campani 1993; Pugliese 1991). Most investigations of Italian views thus remain limited to opinion polls and questionnaires (e.g., Bonifazi 1992; Italia-razzismo 1990; Sciortino 1993), and analyses of popular culture and the media (e.g., Bocca 1988; CENSIS 1990b; Gallini 1989, 1992; Mansoubi 1990; Marletti 1989).

The research

This study addresses the hitherto neglected question of everyday European responses to immigrants. It is based on fieldwork conducted briefly in 1988 and for most of 1990 in Palermo, supplemented with travel throughout Sicily and trips to Rome and Florence. The project initially sought to provide an ethnographic perspective on the notion that working people are structurally inclined by their insecurity to express "working-class racism" or a class-specific hostility towards immigrants (Phizacklea and Miles 1979, 1980). Over the course of research I sought to learn more about how class and culture shape Sicilian views of immigrants by including members of the bourgeoisie in the study. At the same time, well-publicized violence and political attacks on immigrants in the Italian north led me to compare regional variations in the politicization of race and immigration in Italy.

A leitmotif of this study is the necessity of integrating the local context into analyses of European reactions to immigrants. In the case of the research site, a large immigrant population, coupled with a shortage of steady employment, would seem to fulfill important conditions for an anti-immigrant backlash. In contrast to the countryside, where mostly African male workers live and work on isolated farms, the various immigrant groups of the city live and sometimes work alongside the local working classes. The issue of state intervention on behalf of immigrants, admittedly in its infancy in 1990, is also relevant because many Sicilians, especially the poor, see the political system as corrupt and hostile to their interests. Like many other Europeans at the beginning of the 1990s, Sicilians worried about how immigrants would affect their security in an increasingly "integrated" Europe, where the freedom of capital receives priority over the maintenance of current consumption standards and social services. In short, when I arrived in Sicily there was good reason to anticipate immigrants being seen as troublesome if not as an outright competitive threat.

The experience of anti-southernism and the history of emigration complicate this expectation. Many Sicilians see themselves as the victims of "Roman" or government indifference and northern Italian economic exploitation as well as prejudice – if not racism. This is closely linked to emigration. In the period 1951–61, about one million of the 1,800,000 southern emigrants moved to the north, among them about 220,000 Sicilians (Renda 1989: 129). Sicilians often recall how southerners in the industrial north-west of Italy were confined to the bottom of the labor market, denied opportunities and services, and stigmatized as *terroni* (plural; singular, *terrone*). *Terrone* encapsulates the stereotype of the lazy, rude, and dangerous southerner (Douglass 1983; Fofi 1964). Sicilian personal experience, national attitude surveys, and political trends in the north indicate that this mean-spirited anti-southernism still thrives, despite the substantial material gains made by southern immigrants. Sicilians whose work takes them north tell of overhearing colleagues there deride them as "blacks" and "Africans." Surveys of Italian opinions regarding immigration show that northerners consistently see southerners as more objectionable than any foreign immigrant population (Colucci *et al.* 1989; Frigessi 1989). Racist graffiti and gang violence in the north often target *terroni* and foreigners alike. Non-traditional political parties such as the Lombard League have also exploited anti-southernism for political gain by tying their not unjustified attack on the corruption of the Italian state to the southerners who supposedly operate the state for their exclusive benefit.

Sicilian understandings of exploitation and marginality bear on their views of newcomers. Some, particularly working people, see immigration as contributing to competition for scarce jobs and inadequate services; as such, immigration represents for them but the last in a series of hardships attributable to north/south inequality, aided and abetted by Rome. Yet identification with a strong regional culture and history, albeit one stigmatized at the national level, makes Sicilians skeptical of the kind of anti-immigrant politics common throughout Europe that vilifies immigrants as threats to national cultural, if not racial, homogeneity. As the "blacks" and "Africans" of Italy, moreover, Sicilians confront the western discourse on race from the ambiguous position of being "black" in relation to Italy's north but "white" in relation to new immigrants. This ambiguity certainly does not inoculate Sicilians against racism, as some Sicilians would hope, but it does complicate the question of race and discrimination. Finally, the experience of emigration is central to Sicilian interpretations of immigrants. While working people understand the hardship that causes and accompanies immigration, it is the bourgeoisie, in particular, and the representatives of churches, unions, and organizations who see former emigrants as duty-bound to fight racism and promote the harmonious integration of immigrants in Sicily.

Because I sought to chart working-class reactions to Africans and Asians, I settled in Albergheria. The cityscape of this and other quarters in old Palermo is a dank maze of alleys and crumbling palaces, hovels, historic churches, empty lots, small shops, and the occasional modern apartment building. Most of the residents have known no other condition than poverty, and not without reason do they distrust outsiders and the government. Following the dictates of ethnographic method, I sought to understand the Albergherians' view of their world by living with them and participating in local life. Some Sicilian friends, hearing of my intention to settle there, warned me of the dangers and inconveniences of my plan. My entry into this rather insular community was facilitated by the sponsorship of a local priest who enjoyed widespread respect for the establishment of a social center. Because Sicilians celebrate the family and dote on young children, the presence of my wife and baby boy also did much to lower neighborhood defenses. My wife, an anthropologist with long experience in matters Sicilian, quickly established a rapport with the local women, who were pleasantly impressed with her knowledge of Sicilian cuisine but remained skeptical of American childrearing practices. My blond and blue-eyed son provoked mock debates as to which baby advertisement he most resembled. While young men pinched and poked him to an angry reaction, young girls and women cuddled and comforted him. We eventually learned to allot a good quarter of an hour to such greetings when leaving the house for appointments elsewhere.

My first practical step to the goal of establishing relations of trust in Alberghería was to become a known quantity. On morning shopping rounds we staggered purchases in order to visit as many shops as possible. We visited with people and gladly accepted their efforts at helping us cope with the contingencies of neighborhood life. They showed us how to deal with a water shortage which left the area without water save for short bursts every other morning. On other occasions they insisted that we buy a long and rather expensive piece of sturdy cloth. This we dutifully wove between the vertical poles of our balcony railing, thus protecting my wife's virtue from the prying eyes of males four stories below. We dropped in at the social center to talk with neighborhood people and volunteers from the middle-class areas beyond. Afternoons, we staved off the relentless sun under the awning of a nearby ice-cream shop. Evenings would often find me out in the street – the proper place for the Sicilian male – and my wife and child at or near to home. There I would join the groups of men standing in piazzas or along side streets, and field questions about politics, sports, and gender relations in the United States. Whenever possible, I steered talk towards the subjects of work possibilities, local politics, emigration, and immigration. Occasionally, I walked several blocks to drink beer and talk with immigrants from North and West Africa about their aspirations and experiences in Italy. Or I would idly stand by and watch immigrant–Sicilian interactions.

After about six months, I felt I had gained sufficient credibility to request formal interviews. Significantly, several assented by remarking that I was clearly a serious researcher and not a "journalist," their term for a muckraker bent on embellishing the already unwholesome reputation of the neighborhood. "Just write the facts and tell your readers that we are people just like everyone else," urged one interviewee. In all, I conducted in-depth, structured interviews with fifteen Albergherians and their families. These lasted from two to eight hours and covered family and employment history, the job market, local politics, emigration, and immigration. I drew on these interviews to formulate a three-page questionnaire (see the Appendix). To gain an idea about the representativeness of the interview group, I gave the questionnaire to fifteen other residents in addition. I also visited a school I call "Garibaldi," located in Zisa, a newer working-class neighborhood outside the old city, where I gave the questionnaire to several classes of returning young adult students in pursuit of an equivalency degree.

In chapter 2 I discuss working-class reactions to Africans and Asians. A review of the local political economy and working Palermitans' views of their place in it forms the background to the presentation. I find working people in Albergheria and Zisa concerned with the prospect of competing with immigrants for scarce jobs and government attention. Few, however, view immigrants as naturally constituted and inferior groups or condone their exploitation; and few blame Palermo's considerable problems on immigrants or seem disposed to support anti-immigrant politics. Working-class appraisals of immigrants are, in general, profoundly ambivalent. As former emigrants, working Palermitans sympathize with those who have left home to secure a tolerable present and a better future. As disparaged *terroni* they understand the stigmatization immigrants sometimes feel. They know that immigrants generally take only those jobs which Sicilians refuse; and when they hire immigrants, they appreciate the reliability and cheapness of these new workers. Yet working Palermitans exaggerate the negative effect of immigrant employment and rail at any comparison of themselves with immigrants. They deny that immigrants will contribute to Italy through their labor and culture as Sicilian emigrants have contributed to the Italian north, Germany, and the United States. They also portray immigrants as undeserving of the attention of the Italian government – attention which they believe should by rights be given to the national working class. In short, their ambivalence is the product of a complex dialectic of class position and self-hatred in which the idioms and realities of competition predominate over those of solidarity. This suggests that blanket claims of working-class racism overlook pertinent issues such as local culture and experience.

Toward the end of the year I also sought comparative data on the reactions of bourgeois Palermo to immigration. While working people live and perhaps work alongside immigrants, the professionals whom I had come to know considered Africans and Asians as reliable and fashionable servants. In countless conversations I had been struck by the ways they gave a Sicilian expression to the anti-racism typical of educated Italians. Drawing on important moments in Sicilian history – the prosperous Arab rule and the Norman policy of tolerating other ethnic groups during the medieval period, the modern experience of emigration – they saw good reasons for accepting immigrants in Sicily. Accordingly, I supplemented impressions gleaned from a snowball sample of friends and acquaintances by giving the questionnaire to two groups of students, one from the University of Palermo, the other from one of the city's best classical high schools (*liceo classico*), which I call Ruggero II.

Conversations and questionnaire results show that members of the bourgeoisie generally express an unproblematic acceptance of "immigrants of color" if not an explicit anti-racism. As I describe in chapter 3, students in both groups denounce racism and support the project of a pluralistic Italy in which immigrants and Italians live free from racial division. These views draw on what I call "paradigms of solidarity," rooted in the ideologies of religious universalism and leftist internationalism, which hold an influential place in postwar Italian political culture. In particular, they seize on ideas developed by the Sicilian intelligentsia concerning the duty of former emigrants to accept new immigrants. In contrast to the inconsistency and ambivalence of working-class accounts, these students' views express sophisticated political ideologies. By broadening the analysis to include members of the bourgeoisie in general, I found these ideals to be contradicted by the economic dominance over foreign workers, particularly female domestic servants, as well as by ideas about the relative aptitude of different immigrant groups. While working people live without incident with those whom they hesitate to consider their equals, the bourgeoisie lament the racial stigmatization of their servants.

This study ends with a consideration of the processes by which immigration and related issues have become politicized in Italy. Parallel to participant-observation in Albergheria, I interviewed representatives of all the pertinent major churches, unions, and cultural associations in Palermo (and some elsewhere). I noted their practical efforts in aid of Africans and Asians, as well as their attempts to pursue a multicultural society within the Sicilian context. Some, pointing to continuing anti-southernism and attacks on immigrants in the north, contrasted a tolerant south with an intolerant north. Using newspaper accounts and discussions with scholars, I attempted to chart the uneven politicization of race and immigration.

Chapter 4 examines concerned institutions and associations in Palermo and compares their politics with those in the north. In contradiction to ideas of Sicilian tolerance, a review of events in 1990 shows that the exploitation of foreign workers as well as violence against them occurs throughout the country. At the same time the review lends a certain credence to Sicilian claims. Not only is anti-immigrant political mobilization confined to the north – but so too are fascist-style violence and intimidation against immigrants and even their Italian supporters. In Sicily, by contrast, a pro-integration agenda characterizes the rather limited political activity on the issue of immigration. The northern-based Lombard League draws on anger towards the Italian state and widespread anti-southernism to demonize immigrants and southerners alike, at the same time as government programs and institutional activity places immigrants at the center of political debate. A stifling patronage system in Sicily and the rest of the south, by contrast, thwarts political expression of popular opinions, including those on immigrants. I argue that this suppression of political expression, as much as the everyday Sicilian acceptance of immigrants, accounts for the absence of anti-immigrant politics in Sicily.

In chapter 5, I return to working-class and bourgeois Palermitans and their views of African and Asian immigrants. I suggest that studying the specific cultural, ideological, and political–economic contexts of everyday European responses to immigration is essential for an understanding of race and racism.

2

When the bottom looks down: working-class views of immigrants in Palermo

The question of working-class racism

This chapter examines the form, content, and extent of racism and other reactions towards Africans and Asians among working Palermitans. Observers agree that, of all groups, European workers reveal the most hostility towards immigrants (Balibar 1991c, 1991e; Castles and Kosack 1985; Husbands 1983; Reeves 1983; Van Dijk 1987; Wieviorka 1992). Trade union representatives, for example, regularly find themselves caught between their aspirations to international solidarity of labor and the protectionist and nationalist demands of their indigenous members (Castles 1984; Grillo 1985). Yet little direct research on the problem has been carried out because most scholars, concentrating on the benefits to capitalists of a racially divided labor force, have too often reduced race to class and overlooked or dismissed the possiblity of racism from below (Roediger 1991: 6–11). However, the few studies to have investigated the ways in which class shapes views on immigrants and essentialist ideologies suggest valuable lines of inquiry.

In their study of a London neighborhood, Annie Phizacklea and Robert Miles (1979, 1980) argue that "working-class racism" derives not so much from adherence to ideologies of racial inequality as from the daily experience of competing with immigrants for jobs and public housing. For the English workers, the visible "coloureds" thus appear as the cause of what are in fact broader trends of industrial decline and rising unemployment. This "racist explanation for material disadvantage and decline," it is important to note, "is only one of a number of explanations which are often as vague and inconsistent as the former" (Phizacklea and Miles 1980: 176). While the authors show how ideology is tied to everyday experience, they cleave too closely to the idea that actual competition over material resources alone causes bitterness and racism. In fact, workers in rich areas of Europe and the United States similarly see immigrants as threatening because their presence underlines the insecurity of native workers in capitalist economies. The validity of local experience in the London study is unfortunately minimized by the lack of attention paid to the ambivalence of working-class views and by the treatment of ideology as false consciousness (Rattansi 1992). A more complete analysis would situate workers' views of self and other in specific cultural and political–economic contexts of postcolonial, postindustrial Europe (Balibar 1991e; Cohen 1992; Wieviorka 1992).

My research in Palermo aimed to provide an ethnographic perspective on these insights. In examining workers' attitudes and actions towards Africans and Asians I sought answers to four broad questions: (1) What are the principal features of political and economic life in Palermo and how do working people see their place in them? (2) To what extent do immigrants pose a competitive threat to working Palermitans in terms of important resources such as jobs, housing, and services? (3) Do Palermitans regard immigrants primarily in racial and racist terms? (4) In what ways does the immigrant presence constitute a perceived threat to workers' status – as workers, as Sicilians, and as white Europeans? Utilizing as a background studies on the large-scale trends in migration and racialization, I focus on the role of working-class experience, including local history and culture, in the formation of Sicilian workers' views on immigrants.

To anticipate the findings of the chapter, in the underdeveloped economy of Palermo the majority of the population struggle to make ends meet with discontinuous sources of income. They remain excluded from all but the lowest rungs of a patronage system through which resources, especially state monies, are often distributed. Because I argue that workers' interpretations of immigrants hinge on their self-evaluations and class consciousness, I describe their notions of self-worth and their own perceptions of their place at the bottom of Sicilian and Italian society. Working Palermitans' awareness of their marginality finds contradictory expression: they reject exploitation as unjust, but also accept their position as the result of their own shortcomings. Despite prevalent material scarcity, large numbers of immigrants do not appear to have posed a direct threat to the welfare of Sicilian workers. Rather, Sicilians and immigrants tend to work in different kinds of jobs, with those held by locals generally enjoying greater pay and security. Working Palermitans recognize this and reject as humiliating the low-status jobs "fit" for immigrants. This understanding rarely finds expression in racial or racist ideas. Working Palermitans distinguish between Africans and Asians with inconsistent and vague terminology; most reject assertions of white supremacy, and few blame their problems on immigrants. Moreover, they recognize that, like themselves, immigrants suffer injustices at the hands of politicians, the mafia, and employers. They empathize with newcomers who, like countless Sicilians, leave family and home behind in search of a modest improvement in their life chances.

The idioms of solidarity, however, are countered and often overwhelmed by idioms of competition and threat. Hounded by insecurity and inconsequence, many working Palermitans see immigrants as competitors for jobs and the attentions of the government. Consequently, at the same time as they describe immigrants as "just like us" they insist that they lower wages, "take the bread from our mouths," and are incapable of contributing to Italy in the way Italian emigrants contributed to their new homelands. I argue that working-class experience shapes this profoundly ambivalent or contradictory view of foreigners. The workings of class and local culture show the complexity beneath broad statements about working-class racism. While the reactions of working Palermitans cannot be severed from their local context, their evaluations do point up key issues in the responses of western European workers to immigration. In closing, I reflect on how the dynamics of working-class self-hatred, the labor market, and the state shape an ideological portrayal of immigrants as threatening.

Political–economic background
Several features of political and economic life in Palermo bear on this study. As many observers have noted, the most striking feature of the city's economy is the lack of stable employment, as evidenced by low rates of formal labor-force participation, high rates of underemployment and unemployment, and rampant undocumented employment, or *lavoro nero* (Banco di Sicilia 1987; Chubb 1982; Guarrasi 1978). Lack of work is linked to a structural imbalance characteristic of underdevelopment throughout the Italian south. In the secondary sector, manufacturing activity, always weak, is the work of a plethora of small, undercapitalized firms, mostly in clothing and shoe-making, woodworking, and metalworking. Facing constant pressure from northern Italian and foreign products, these firms survive, when they do, by tapping abundant reserves of cheap and non-unionized labor. Similar firms predominate in construction, where cyclical demand exacerbates these tendencies.

The tertiary sector increasingly drives the urban economy. Whereas the secondary sector accounted for 35 percent of employment and the tertiary 59 percent in 1971, by 1981 the latter had risen to 69 percent while the former had fallen to 27 percent (Banco di Sicilia 1987). The hypertrophied tertiary sector in turn reflects the primacy of the public sector in the absence of meaningful private-sector development. In Palermo, the public sector includes countless public and semi-public agencies linked to municipal, provincial, regional, and national governments. (According to one agency, 35.6 percent of the city's workforce in the early 1970s was made up of public employees, broadly defined [Chubb 1982: 46].) Commercial and service firms replicate secondary-sector trends. Here, too, a few large concerns contrast with myriad small, often family, businesses which enjoy state subsidies, and with street vendors, both unlicensed and licensed. Complicating the analysis of economic trends is the significant, if unquantifiable, economic activity in drug traffic, construction, and other activity associated with the mafia.

The underdeveloped economy is linked to a basically tripartite class structure, consisting of a bourgeoisie proper, a petty bourgeoisie, and a large and heterogeneous working population. The small *alta borghesia* ("upper bourgeoisie") of landowners, heads of large firms, and professionals, in particular, made up 6.7 percent of the active poulation in 1981. The considerable power of this class is based not on industry but on real estate and construction interests and control of state monies. The larger *piccola borghesia* ("petty bourgeoisie") enjoy middle and steady income levels, either as white-collar employees or as owner-operators of independent businesses. As throughout the south, massive public spending has underwritten the expansion of the middle classes, whether directly through public administration or indirectly through increased demand for services and commerce (Sylos Labini 1974). In 1981, this class made up fully 51 percent of Palermo's active population, compared with 45 percent for the province of Palermo and 44 percent for the region of Sicily, a difference reflecting the concentration of administrative jobs in Palermo (Banco di Sicilia 1987: Table 1:12).

Making up the majority of the urban population, working people account for about half of formal employment and most of the considerable volume of informal activity. A defining feature of the working-class condition is small and discontinuous income. This broad definition is consistent with Vincenzo Guarrasi's (1978) notion of the "marginal condition," which includes the three strata of the proletariat proper, the lowest levels of the petty bourgeoisie, and paupers on the basis of low and discontinuous income. Guarrasi uses the inclusive term "marginal," rather than the contrasting ones of "proletariat"/"lumpen," to underline the significance of unstable employment in the capitalist labor market, particularly in Palermo, where small, traditional, and non-unionized firms rely on cheap and flexible labor inputs. I agree with Guarrasi's characterization of the class structure in Palermo but prefer the term "working people" or "working classes" to connote shared experiences and expectations.

The fluidity of survival strategies adopted by the poor is captured in the phrases *mille mestieri* ("thousand trades") and *l'arte di arrangiarsi* ("the art of getting by"). The temporary nature of employment, the variety of occupations, and the incidence of "refuge" activity in the informal sector and in criminal activities make any understanding of marginal work impressionistic. The range of activities is bewildering and includes, among others, services, petty commerce, manufacturing in small shops and at home, scavenging scrap metal and cardbroad, and illegal activity such as theft and the sale of contraband. In the course of a year a male head of household might enjoy the rare pleasure of securing a steady job with benefits. Another might move from construction to woodworking to a city-sponsored training program (*cantiere*) to selling clothes at weekly markets. A poorer man still might engage in unlicensed street vending of fruits and vegetables, scrap scavenging, and perhaps try his hand as an *ariffatore*, running a neighborhood lottery. Their wives might work part-time cleaning homes and offices. Child labor also plays an important role in the survival strategies of the very poor; it is not uncommon for many children to fail to complete the eighth grade (that is, the third year of secondary school – *terza media*), because their families depend on their income. As Thomas Belmonte found in Naples, survival "for the poor involves continuous effort but discontinuous success" (Belmonte 1989: 112).

Application of the concept of patronage offers insight into the workings of political–economic trends in Palermo, including class relations. Patronage, also known as clientelism, is a form of unequal exchange between "patrons" and "clients," characterized by long-term dyadic ties, informality, and the idioms of friendship and kinship (Schmidt 1977). In Palermo, this means that when looking for a "favor," who you know and what you offer them often counts for more than what you know or can do. Thus an unemployed man receives a place in a *cantiere* program in the place of another thanks to an official whose memory of a mutual friend has been jogged by the receipt of an envelope containing a bribe, the infamous *bustarella*. Or a bank manager sees fit to hire the son of a cousin who years earlier intervened on his behalf in a troublesome legal case.

In short, key resources are distributed through patronage networks. In the context of economic underdevelopment, the elephantine public sector constitutes a major patronage asset. For most of the postwar period, the Christian Democratic party (DC – Democrazia Cristiana) has enjoyed almost complete hegemony over politics in southern Italy. In Palermo, the DC early on transformed the public sphere "into a powerful political machine for the advancement of personal and party fortunes" (Chubb 1982: 70). DC leaders effected this transformation in collusion with various elite families and members of mafia families, or *cosche*.[1]

The chaotic urban expansion of the late 1950s and early 1960s exemplifies the subjugation of the many to the few. At that time "New Palermo" surged north-west from the old city center, cementing over the citrus groves and farms of the lush coastal plain, Conca d'Oro, that surrounds the city. Through manipulation of zoning instruments, building permits, contracts for public construction projects, and credit institutions, the DC elite secured enduring power and made fortunes for itself, its associates, and known mafiosi. Out of the logic of speculation grew a chaotic cityscape. Countless violations of restrictions on building height and the unauthorized conversion of many public spaces (e.g., schools, parks, parking facilities) into private property resulted in very high population densities, inadequate infrastructures, and interminable traffic jams. At the same time, the city administration allowed the old city to wither from neglect. From 1951 to 1979, the population of the center declined from 125,271 to an estimated 40,000 (Quilici 1980: 31, 107–8), as residents moved out or were transferred to the vast public housing estates on the city's northern periphery. Those remaining in the old city endured few services, scandalously poor housing conditions, and the neglect of City Hall.

Several consequences of the patronage system merit attention. For the populace, bad government is palpable and distressingly familiar, taking the form of: generally poor and selectively provided services; a bloated, inefficient, and corrupt bureaucracy; a deteriorating historic center; unregulated urbanization; inadequate infrastructures; and chronic yet avoidable water shortages. Sicilian scholars have called Palermo *la città spunga* ("the sponge city") to stress its capacity to absorb immense amounts of public money without showing a discernible effect (Crisantino 1990). In essence, patronage in southern Italy constitutes a form of class relations, where the power of the patrons rests on their ability to control and restrict the distribution of resources (White 1980). Underdevelopment, in this context, is favorable because it insures the primacy of the public-sector power base of patrons; likewise, bureacratic inefficiency guarantees the importance of mediation (Chubb 1982). In a context of modernized tastes and expectations in the absence of economic development (Schneider *et al.* 1972), patrons are always in demand.

Also key to patronage is the perversion of public participation in politics. As a mass-based party in a modern democracy, the DC relies on numerical support in the form of votes. However, votes in this context express not support for a party platform but real or hoped-for admittance to the party's patronage apparatus. The essence of this complicated process is the exchange of votes for favors, usually jobs, promotions, bureaucratic mediation in the case of the bourgeoisie, and food and promises of jobs in the case of working people. This takes place among the bourgeoisie through friendly relations, usually at the workplace, and in poorer areas through an extensive network of local bosses. The commanding grip on the body politic-economic by the DC and the implication of many Palermitans in patronage networks long impeded reform movements.

The anti-mafia movement provides a rare example of a broad-based political mobilization for reform. The ongoing movement consists of the Coordinamento Antimafia, an umbrella organization founded in 1988, reform-minded politicians from the DC and opposition parties, and members of recently founded social centers working among the poor. The movement was formed in response to the bloody mafia wars of the early 1980s and a related series of murders of state officials, the so-called "excellent cadavers." The movement criticizes not only the mafia's reign of terror but the patronage system itself, epitomized by the DC machine but symptomatic of Sicilian society as a whole and of Italian politics in general. Leaders speak of the necessity of making a clean "break" (*spaccatura*) with the current system of "affiliation" to party and patron, which is to be replaced by the "transparency" of the rule of law.

The successes of the anti-mafia struggle are many and include scholarly analyses and conferences, public protests, and the gains of the "Palermo Spring" (1986–7) during the heady early years of the administration of DC reformer Leoluca Orlando. By the time of this research the transformative powers of the movement were severely compromised by rearguard actions in City Hall, the portrayal of activists as anti-Sicilian careerists, and the brazen attacks by the mafia on recalcitrant officials. The weakness of the movement also derived from widespread involvement in patronage networks. As Jane and Peter Schneider have written of the Coordinamento's strident call for a complete break with clientelism:

Innocent and morally compelling on the surface, this assault threatened the schools, the professions, the public sector jobs and construction variances that constitute the "resource bundles" of all the unpropertied classes in Palermo – including the intelligentsia.   (*Schneider and Schneider 1997*)[2]

The consequences of patronage extend to the realm of public culture. The emphasis on coalitions and dyadic ties among friends and (fictive) kin resonates with the cultural code of hospitality and the elaboration of friendship in which the distinction between business and social associations becomes blurred. To have many friends, especially if they are well placed, is to enjoy potential business associates. Patronage also promotes the possibility of individual gain at the expense of collective degradation – as exemplified by recent urban expansion. This bears on the celebration in southern Italy of *furbizia*, individual "cunning" and "cleverness" (Belmonte 1989; Schneider and Schneider 1976). If people extoll the *furbo*, they pity and ridicule the *fesso,* or "fool." One's ability to pursue one's own interests is enhanced by the general disregard for the government, whose integrity is considered to be paper thin. Such an attitude takes all-too-common expression in the contempt for the commonweal and in celebrations of brazen arrogance (*prepotenza*). The immobilism and corruption of the system also generate apathy and disillusionment, at the same time as pervasive organized crime breeds fear and a cautious attitude of keeping to one's own affairs.

Working-class experience and class consciousness
The forces already outlined find painful expression in working-class areas of old and new Palermo. Poor housing conditions, failing services, high rates of disease, poverty, chronic underemployment and unemployment, child labor, low educational attainment, and numerous informal activities shading into crime describe harsh living conditions in working-class neighborhoods, or *quartieri popolari* (Crisantino 1990). A study conducted in 1988–9 in Albergheria by a local social center, Centro Sociale San Francesco Saverio (CSSS 1990), found that 20 percent of the school-age children had dropped out of school and another 40 percent were behind. The study describes an alarming incidence (93 cases) of homeless children, *ragazzi per la strada*, without education or employment (CSSS 1990: 263–9). Allied bombing during World War II and the erosive agents of time and neglect have left the quarter and most of the old city in tatters. The occasional modern or well-maintained apartment stands out against a background of abandoned buildings, makeshift artisans' workshops, crumbling palaces, tiny stores, rubble-strewn lots, and makeshift shacks.

Some narrow streets are made darker still by the beams which span them, bracing weak facades that might otherwise crumble. Out of 675 people interviewed by CSSS (Centro Sociale San Francesco Saverio) researchers, 20 percent live in housing in danger of collapse and another 40 percent occupy housing of very poor quality. Yet boisterous outdoor life, street-side craft activity, shops, and the sprawling, ancient open-air market of nearby Ballarò offset to some extent the general degradation. With its bewildering variety and volume, hawkers' cries and bustling crowds, the market animates the quarter and lends it a theatrical air.

Like the residents of Albergheria, the working population of Zisa, whose student population I also studied, finds itself at the margins of political and economic life in Palermo. Built up during the postwar construction boom, Zisa is located near the western edge of the city. The buildings, though of recent construction, are drab and neglected. The emptiness of the wide streets contrasts with the activity of old city neighborhoods such as Albergheria.

Most residents in Albergheria and Zisa belong to the working classes. In a study conducted in the late 1970s, Guarrasi classified 26.4 percent of Albergheria's population as petty bourgeoisie, 8.2 percent as workers, 16.6 percent as marginalized proletarians, and 43 percent as paupers (Guarrasi 1980: 78–9). The CSSS study describes an analogous situation ten years later: only 26 percent of the adult men and 5.8 percent of the adult women hold steady jobs (CSSS 1990: 208–9). Similarly, questionnaire responses among returning adult students in Zisa show that only 35 percent hold steady jobs and that half of these are undocumented. In both Albergheria and Zisa there exists a small population of steadily employed artisans, shop keepers, and salaried employees. However, for most, steady and documented jobs with benefits are scarce, particularly with the recent decline in construction. In the absence of steady work, many household heads practice the art of getting by, taking a succession of usually undocu-mented jobs and making attempts at self-employment, supplemented with some form of assistance from public and religious institutions. Full-time employment for women is rarer still, though some work as cleaners in a local hospital and in homes and offices. Students at what I will call the "Garibaldi" school in Zisa pin their hopes of employment on education. As participants in a nation-wide "150 Hours Course", they can obtain an equivalency diploma for *terza media* (roughly equal to passing the eighth grade in the United States system, or the third year at secondary school). The diploma is the minimum educational requirement for entry into "competitions" (*concorsi*) for valued public-sector jobs.

How do people in Zisa and Albergheria view their situation? Working Palermitans see themselves as hounded by insecurity and humiliated by marginalization. The precariousness of employment is a well-spring of discontent. "Underemployment is Palermo's biggest problem" two young men told me, in unison, and without exaggeration. A man with a rare union job summed up working-class fears this way:

We live in fear, uncertainty, because work is so hard to find. Every morning we get up and make the sign of the cross to thank the Lord for another day. Today your wife puts something in the skillet for lunch, but you can't say that it'll be there tomorrow.

He went on to criticize the unfair, clientelistic distribution of jobs:

Say I've got a university degree and enter a competition, but they give it to a guy with a second grade education as a favor. Where's all my and my family's sacrifices? At sea!

The difficulty of finding and maintaining steady work, the loss of benefits entailed in "black work," the bouts of unemployment, *l'arte di arrangiarsi* – all this dogs the working Palermitan, eats away at his or her self-image, and cultivates a sixth sense for locating work through networks and patrons. The crushing poverty of the popular quarters of Palermo in the 1950s, described by Danilo Dolci (1959), the famous advocate of Sicily's poor in the 1950s and 1960s, has abated; nonetheless, the fundamental insecurity of working-class life remains.

Those who find salaried employment are made vulnerable by the relentless operation of the first rule of market economics, the law of supply and demand. The most obvious way in which employers exploit the surplus of workers to jobs is through "black" or undocumented work. This relationship varies from one of mutual convenience – the employer retains the substantial payments earmarked for pension and other funds and the employee gains unreported income – to one of dominance, in which the employer obtains cheap labor for usually unfulfilled promises of documentation and better pay. By way of example, employers might register the employee only surreptitiously to underpay taxes and benefit payments, thus jeopardizing the employee's pension and accident insurance coverage. This economic relationship is also a personal one, one of dependency and indebtedness, in which the employer presumably does the employee the favor of granting them employment. In such circumstances, for an employee to seek redress at a union office, or even to report for treatment of a work-related injury at the hospital, amounts to a betrayal of that trust and indebtedness. An employer so betrayed fires the ungrateful woman or man and informs other employers of the incident.

Local politicians and mafia figures also plague the working classes. For many in Albergheria, the departure of Leoluca Orlando, the reform-minded mayor of Palermo (1985–90), epitomized the corruption of the political system. His government's assault on corruption and the mafia, as well as his attention to Palermo's poor, won him the undying admiration of the common folk, although his reforms slowed the construction on which poor Palermo has depended heavily since the 1950s. In 1990, Orlando headed the Christian Democratic list and carried the party to a remarkable absolute majority. Despite his receiving a record number of "preferential," or non-binding, votes, which indicate voter preference for a particular candidate, opponents within his party at the local and national levels blocked his re-entry into office. The Christian Democratic leadership eventually gave the mayoralty to the candidate placed twenty-third in preference votes (Codevilla 1992: 148). A neighborhood man voiced the sentiment of many when he concluded from the affair that honest politicians are either corrupted, assassinated, or forced out.

It is by this mafia/politics combination that many working Palermitans explain the manifold degradation of their lives and of the city. It is common knowledge in Palermo that "nothing gets done" (*non si fa niente*) without bribery, friends, and patrons. A young man, unemployed and, with a high-school diploma, well-educated for the quarter, told me about patronage in the famous competitions for jobs in the public sector:

These things are rigged. Say there are fifty jobs and a thousand applicants. Those in charge set aside forty-five jobs for friends, to use as favors, leaving the remaining five to the crowd. It's impossible, but I keep trying since there's nothing else.

Such assertions, though impossible to prove in a systematic way, find ample substantiation in personal experience and gossip. Everyone has heard of jobs secured or telephones installed overnight though bribery or friendship, just as everyone knows that unconnected people such as themselves do not win jobs in competitions. At the same time, this state of affairs almost necessitates a constant search for patrons and forces people to live by their wits.

During my stay in Palermo, a scandal exploded involving *il mago di Villabate*. A "sorcerer" from a nearby town was said to be able to double investors' money in a matter of weeks, owing to shrewd investment; indeed, during the initial weeks of the game he actually repaid investors handsome profits. Many working Palermitans lost thousands when the pyramid scheme finally collapsed. When a neighbor told me of losing several thousand dollars to the sorcerer, I asked why he of all people, the man who had warned me of the countless subterfuges mastered by Palermitans, did not see through the scam. He startled me by saying that of course he knew it was a pyramid scheme; his only regret was not having been *furbo* enough to have invested his money earlier and thereby profited from others' misfortune. I then recalled what another man had told me about the essence of the mafia: "To profit from the misery of others, what we call *maccagno* in Sicilian, is terrible. For me, this is mafia, this is power."

In popular perception, nonetheless, it is the hostile national government in Rome, perhaps allied to northern big business, that somehow perpetuates the plague of unemployment. It is common to hear that the "real mafia" is up north – in the political capital, Rome, and in the financial capital, Milan. "Italy is a democratic republic founded on work," a young man said, quoting the first sentence of the Italian constitution; but, he complained, despite unemployment here the government does nothing. This, in turn, channels frustrated young men into petty crime and the mafia; they are the ever ready *mano d'opera* ("manual laborers") of the mafia, one told me. Another threw up his hands, saying "Shit! There's a waiting list to get into the mafia!" The resulting order is reprehensible to many. The tradesman who described the exploitation of insecurity as the essence of mafia also lamented the fate of the three-month workshops instituted by Orlando to provide relief to the poor who had lost work when the crackdown on the mafia halted much construction. Without bribing the officials at the employment office, he claimed, it was hard if not impossible to obtain a position in one of these workshops.

Working people bitterly acknowledge their marginality. While they lay the blame for this on the collusion of politicians and the mafia, and to a lesser extent on employers ever ready to exploit the surplus of workers over jobs, they also accept their material and ideological powerlessness. Their obvious subordination – on the labor market, in politics, in cultural evaluations – proves to them, in a persistent way, their own inferiority. The conclusion they read follows directly both from the logic of money in a capitalist democracy and from the reality of the mafia. In the former logic, the citizen and employee are supposedly free and equal, and will succeed or fail on the basis of merit. In the second logic, the exercise of power generates a form of authority in the absence of a strong state presence – an authority to which people acknowledge their subordination through obedience if not respect.

4. Large mural, Piazza San Francesco Saverio. The mural, painted by A. Guccione and entitled "Rebuilding the City," was painted on the occasion of a 1987 neighborhood reclamation project (the "Olympics") organized by the Centro Sociale San Francesco Saverio. The artist draws on Sicilian folk images of the heroic Norman era to depict the contemporary effort to reclaim Palermo's *centro storico* from its degraded state. The mural dates to the "Palermo Spring," a period of enthusiatic reform associated with the first years of the administration of mayor Leoluca Orlando.

The brutality permeating life among the poor is an expression of the frustration born of living out this powerlessness. Domestic violence against women and children occurs with alarming frequency. "It is the rule of the strongest here," a volunteer at the Social Center told me. I recalled a bizarre scene I had witnessed several months earlier. Four boys were playing with a soccer ball, but they were not passing the ball around or playing a game; instead the largest boy had lined the others against a wall and was calmly, methodically, kicking the ball at them. As Belmonte observes of the Neapolitan poor: "The brutality of the poor is learned. It imitates the brutality of class" (Belmonte 1989: 102).

To some extent, the activity of the Social Center in Albergheria (and perhaps the "150 Hour Course" at the Garibaldi school in Zisa) offers people the possibility of conceptualizing counter-hegemonic ideals of merit and of initiating political action. The Social Center, founded in 1986 during the "Palermo Spring" – a period of reform associated with the first years of the administration of mayor Leoluca Orlando – includes a church, an ex-monastery (renovated to include a local public-health office), a cinema, and a cooperative restaurant (*trattoria*). Although headed by a priest and housed in a church, it is "non-denominational" (*aconfessionale*) and "not affiliated with political parties" (*apartitico*) in character. According to its brochure, the center's members:

have created and maintain a *democratic* "space" of cultural, economic, social, recreational initiatives, programmed and realized in total and sincere *pluralism*, convinced that religious and ideological differences should be accepted and utilized as occasions for enrichment and complementarity rather than for polemics and division.[3]   (*CSSS nd: 1*)

In the short history of the Social Center, its organizers have distinguished themselves through both community programs and participation in the intellectual and political movement against corruption and the mafia in Palermo (see, for example, Cavadi 1990; Schneider and Schneider 1997). Activities include: after-school daycare, care for the elderly, a women's group, the health clinic, the restaurant, and a political mobilization for improved housing conditions. Linking the practical and the political is a "theology of reclamation" (*teologia di risanamento*), which endeavors through collaboration to impart to local residents the capacity to recognize and pursue their fundamental rights, to raise their consciousness and self-respect. One of the first young men in the neighborhood to join the Social Center described its principal benefit as the promotion of the novel idea that people are citizens with rights, not merely clients begging for favors.

The "150 Hours" courses at Garibaldi, while primarily aimed at bringing students up to US eighth-grade levels (equivalent to the third year at secondary school) in required subjects, also introduce them to analytic tools for critically examining their environment. Instructors seek to explain the political economy of clientelism in Palermo and how it results in urban degradation and the suppression of political expression. Like the volunteers at the Social Center, teachers at Garibaldi emphasize how ignorance of politics and citizens' rights is a consequence of the current political system and helps reinforce it. With regard to immigration, they relate it to current global patterns of inequality and to other population movements in the past, such as emigration from Sicily. They caution students against anti-immigrant sentiment by noting that as former emigrants they should be sympathetic to the plight of immigrants. They also note that immigrants do not take jobs that Sicilians want, nor do immigrants alter the fundamental injustice of life in Palermo.

The impact of these ideas is hard to gauge, but it is probably not great. Most students are intent only on getting a diploma and do not take the course work seriously, although in each of the four classes I attended some

5. Neighborhood activists. Don Cosimo Scordato (center left), director of the Centro Sociale San Francesco Saverio, with an unidentified man and two young neighborhood men who operate a well-known restaurant associated with the Centro.

students displayed keen insights. Some, for example, understood that the exploitation of immigrants operates in much the same way as their own marginalization. Teachers also admit that students have a hard time grasping the relation of the global and historical inequalities structuring immigration to their lives in Palermo, or in regarding their place at the bottom of Italian society in a critical manner.

Working Palermitans more commonly seek to redress their marginalization through claims to cultural superiority. By portraying themselves as innocent victims of the machinations of the powerful, they lay claim to the moral high ground. They see themselves as virtuous upholders of traditions in culture and language against the shameless and self-righteous modernity of the bourgeoisie. They lampoon inhabitants of the wealthy New Palermo for their inability to speak or even comprehend the "beautiful" local dialect. Working Palermitans also revel in the supposed defects of their own boisterousness and communal street life.

It is above all with regard to proper behavior between men and women – and the accompanying constellation of ideas and practices concerning honor, dishonor, dating, and marriage – that working Palermitans define themselves as dignified bearers of tradition. Against the liberated ways of the bourgeoisie they espouse the ideal of (female) virginity before marriage, and engage in circumscribing the activities of nubile girls. Against cohabitation and informal marriage ceremonies they demand the traditional dowry (*corredo*), the blessing of both parents, long-term engagement, and a formal ceremony. As an artisan, proud to be able to provide a proper marriage for his daughter, told me, "we still know how to do things the right way, to follow tradition" (see Booth 1988 for similar accounts in rural Sicily).

Despite these understandings of their oppression and their counter-assertions of cultural worth, working Palermitans also accept and live with their own debasement. As Thomas Belmonte (1989: 142) says of the poor of Naples: "They have a culture that is simultaneously against poverty, adapted to the stresses of poverty, and mangled by poverty." Palermitans strenuously decry the injustice of the system; but the apportionment of power and the logics of value under capitalism and the mafia translate their subordination into demerit. A local shopkeeper, apparently oblivious to the existence of the Social Center, commented on the gravity of local problems by saying that "we don't need to send missionaries abroad, we need to send them here." According to the analysis of an alert young man associated with the Social Center, administrative neglect, joblessness, and lack of services foster social degradation, in which the destitute lose self-respect, take children out of school to put them to work, and lose interest in the condition of the neighborhood. The Social Center, he concluded, has barely scratched the surface of people's consciousness. Another Social Center volunteer described Albergheria as "two realities: people who have been able to redeem themselves [*si è saputo riscattarsi*] and create a new identity and people who do not succeed in redeeming themselves."

Furthermore, rampant clientelism, undocumented income, and contempt for the state implicate many as participants in the general corruption, even if legitimized in their minds as survival strategies. Sicilians often portray tax evasion as acceptable on the grounds that the government is irresponsible and that it overtaxes Italians in the knowledge that taxes due will never be paid in full. Only a *fesso* would pay all his taxes, while a *furbo* would pay none at all. A man in Albergheria pointed out the hypocrisy in blaming all problems on the government. Without the complicity and avarice of local elites, he said, the national government would be unable to exploit Sicilians. He went on to say that Palermitans of all classes engage in tax evasion and other illegalities.

The shifting, essentially dyadic, organization of patronage networks works against popular political mobilization and produces cynicism and apathy. Guarrasi (1980) observes that major parties and trade and tenants' unions rarely succeed in organizing the residents of Albergheria or in getting them to participate in their organizations on a regular basis. Local cynicism and apathy with regard to political participation was evident in responses to the already noted 1990 protest, organized by the Social Center, for safe public housing for people living in "barracks" or makeshift shacks. Leaders of the Social Center camped in the middle of a piazza as part of the protest. Many local residents grumbled about the inefficiency of such an action, and criticized the foolishness of organizing in support of the "dirt" of the quarter, as one young man called the barracks' residents. Some eventually joined in the protest, and many more were impressed when the event elicited a visit from the new mayor. But few supported the protest or saw it as an example to be followed in a general struggle for expanded services in the neighborhood.

Importantly, these self-proclaimed bearers of authentic culture rarely attain their ideals. The high incidence of teenage pregnancy and elopement, for example, contradicts authentic Sicilian cultural ideals of proper behavior for young women. The poverty of *centro storico* residents means that families often cannot afford proper marriage ceremonies and costly dowries. Some parents pool their resources in order to give one daughter an enviable wedding, while encouraging the others to elope or suppress their desires. High unemployment also means that many prospective grooms fail to meet the requirements of their girlfriend's parents. Guarrasi (1980: 83) quotes a man who had cloistered his daughters from potential suitors: "I prefer to give them a piece of bread myself rather than give them as wives to some unemployed man or cardboard collector from the quarter."[4] Finally, the very phrasing of working people's assertions of authenticity and moral superiority, which represents their culture in opposition to that of the bourgeoisie of New Palermo, belies their recognition of their own marginality to mainstream Palermo and Italian culture. The contradictory and ambivalent nature of these working-class self-appraisals comes to the fore as people interpret the presence and threat of African and Asian newcomers.

The question of competition
Given the difficulty of finding and keeping steady work in Palermo, the recent arrival of thousands of immigrants from Morocco, Tunisia, Senegal, Sri Lanka, the Philippines, Cape Verde, Mauritius, Ghana and elsewhere raises the question of competition. Because most accounts of working-class racism hinge on the question of competition, I begin my

review of working Palermitans' responses to immigrants with an assessment of competition for jobs, housing, and services. In general, I describe
a rarely competitive situation in which Africans and Asians possess the
jobs and housing refused by local poor.

Immigrants find themselves at the bottom of Palermo's highly differen-
tiated labor market. Although a few immigrants work in construction and
manufacturing, most work in the tertiary sector, as domestic servants, in
low-level services, and as self-employed street vendors. In sum, they do the
hardest and lowest-paying jobs in the urban economy. Consonant with
high levels of informal economic activity among the working population
as a whole, immigrant work is typically undocumented in the case of
employees and unlicensed in the case of the self-employed. Within the
context of economic subordination, however, there are important differences in job type and security.

Immigrant labor-market participation varies significantly by sex and
national origin. Predominantly female immigrants from Asia and West
Africa work almost to a woman as domestics (*colf*) for the bourgeoisie in
New Palermo. Many early immigrants found jobs through missionaries
active in their home countries, such as the Salesians, while others found
jobs through employment agencies or employers themselves. This situation was the product of both a burgeoning bourgeoisie and the declining
availability of the poor local women who had traditionally staffed the
homes of the rich. Crushing poverty had forced many poor women in the
past to seek domestic work even though they regarded it as shameful; particularly compromised was the live-in maid, whose honor and virginity
were considered imperiled by her distance from kinsmen and unsupervised
isolation with her employer. From the late 1960s, increasing state supports
and greater employment opportunities often related to the urban expansion enabled most poor Sicilian women in the *centro storico* to reject
domestic work, at least on a full-time basis. Today, foreign women occupy
virtually all the full-time positions in the sector, both live-in and live-out.
Those who lack a full-time job tend to receive lower wages; they patch
together a living with a combination of temporary, part-time positions. By
contrast, those Sicilian women who still work in the domestic sector work
only on an occasional or part-time basis to supplement family income, as
noted.

Two church-related associations currently act as placement centers for
foreign and local domestic workers, and provide such services as legal
assistance and job training. The Palermo branch of the national Associazione Professionale Italiana delle Collaboratrici Familiari (API–COLF –

Italian Professional Association of Family Helpers), associated with the Salesian order, processes about one thousand requests for employees yearly. The smaller Centro La Speranza/ACLI–COLF is a division of the national Associazioni Cristiane Lavoratori Italiani (ACLI), a national Christian workers' association. Both associations report that job offers exceed the number of applicants. They also note a change in working conditions for foreigners. In the past, foreign women, particularly those working as live-in maids, were often underpaid and exploited by employers who held their undocumented status against them. Today, most of these workers possess residence and work permits, and receive the going pay rate, which as in most Italian cities is above the national minimum standard and varies by skill. In the end, immigrants are hired not only because they are cheaper, which at times they may not be, but because they are more reliable and willing. A loose ranking of domestic workers exists wherein prestige and skill bring higher wages, increased job security, and benefits. Filipinos, here as elsewhere in Italy and Europe, occupy the most advantageous position. They owe their status to several factors: they confer on employers a certain enviable elegance as well-educated, exotic, and dependable servants, who, as one of the first immigrant groups to Palermo, are familiar with Italian and Italian ways. They are followed by Cape Verdians, Mauritians, Sri Lankans (both men and women), and finally Ghanaians. I return to the question of the domestic hierarchy at the end of chapter 3.

While most Asian and some African women work as domestics in the luxury high-rises of New Palermo, most male immigrants work in the poor neighborhoods of the *centro storico* and elsewhere, in which they live. In the center, North Africans (mostly male) and West Africans, like the poorest Sicilians there, conjure up a livelihood out of series of temporary and undocumented, or "black," jobs. The two populations, however, occupy different niches in Palermo's byzantine labor market. Immigrants' jobs are more stigmatized, more often temporary, and pay less. Immigrants work for as little as 3,000–4,000 lire per hour ($2.50 to $3.30 at the 1990 exchange rate of about 1,200 lire per $1.00), while locals start at 6,000 lire per hour. While both groups lack the security and benefits of documented employment, only Sicilians can make a good wage in *lavoro nero*, especially as street and market vendors. Most importantly, perhaps, state supports and family networks enable most working Palermitans to concede to immigrants *i lavori umili* ("humble jobs") such as washing stairs in apartment buildings or washing dishes in restaurants. The more foreigners assume such positions, the more stigmatized they become for Sicilians to perform.

Finally, there are those male immigrants who, as *vu cumprà*, have created an economic niche for themselves as itinerant street vendors of Africana and low-priced seasonal items. These men come from Morocco, Senegal, and occasionally from Tunisia, and move across the city and throughout the country in loose (North African) or tight-knit (Senegalese) groups (on immigrant group organization, see Fortunato and Methnani 1990; Khouma 1990). In Palermo, street vendors, along with the North Africans who brave traffic in the hope of washing car windshields at the rare Palermo stop light, form the most visible part of the immigrant population. Like the "mosquitos," those who wash windshields, the *vu cumprà* are alternately pitied for their misery and scorned as pests. Merchants, in particular, object to these vendors spreading out their wares in front of their stores, but so far there is no evidence of an organized or coordinated protest.

In general, there is a kind of split in which jobs held by working Palermitans and immigrants differ by occupation, pay, and prestige. Sicilians gain more pay and security, while immigrants receive the low-paying and humiliating jobs which Sicilians refuse. Further, because networks and patronage play such a large role in the acquisition of good jobs, as the quotes above (see pp. 34–5) suggested, immigrants, who lack these ties, are not real competitors for them. Competition for jobs is therefore minimal.

A similar differential applies to housing. The majority of foreigners live in the *centro storico*, often in the nearly uninhabitable or condemned apartments left vacant by the recent exodus from the old center. The accommodation of foreigners in the dilapidated center represents the culmination of a logic of degradation in which landlords, retaining title in hope of a future slum-clearance project, do not maintain the buildings that they rent out to a succession of marginal or transient populations such as the local poor, the elderly, university students, and now immigrants (Professor Vincenzo Guarrasi, personal communication). These dwellings often lack basic amenities such as running water, heating, and efficient roofs. Immigrants also find housing in working-class areas outside the old center, such as Borgo and Zisa, where housing conditions are better. Their arrival, moreover, has not provoked a general rise in rents, although immigrants do pay exaggerated rents in all neighborhoods, as the Sicilians admit themselves and the immigrants complain (for similar reports, see Crisantino 1992: 54). Nevertheless, homelessness is rare here, whereas in the north immigrants experience great difficulties in obtaining housing, owing to high rents, the shortage of housing, and the reluctance of Italians to rent to them. As I suggest later, the housing problem has contributed to the image of immigration as a crisis in the north.

As regards services, the undocumented status of most immigrants prior to Law #39 in 1990 made them ineligible for most public benefits, which, like public housing, are in short supply and poorly administered in Palermo. Importantly, even with the new immigration law, immigrants are not eligible for public housing, which is much needed but rarely delivered in Palermo. Many immigrants have instead sought assistance at the Social and Medical Center for Immigrants at the Oratory Santa Chiara. Santa Chiara is located in Ballarò, the neighborhood adjacent to Albergheria. The medical center, often referred to as the *poliambulatorio*, was established in 1988 on the initiative of a student and some of her faculty at the University of Palermo School of Medicine (Mansueto 1989). By 1990 its volunteer staff had treated over 1,000 people. Members of the Salesian Order and volunteers also assist immigrants and local poor. They regularly open Santa Chiara to immigrant associations and initiatives, such as the Tamil school, established in 1990.

Immigrant and working-class Sicilian participation on the Palermo labor market, and the apportionment of services and housing, is in sum essentially non-competitive. There is a complicated dual labor market, one side of which is occupied by nationals and the other by foreigners, among whom participation varies by nationality. Many commentators have seen job competition as the cause of working-class anger over immigration, but this resentment can also feed off the protectionism and hierarchy of dual labor markets. The division of workers among discrete and ranked labor-market niches, the ensuing wage differentials, absence of collective experience, and jockeying for position through union agreements have been shown to fuel ethnic and racial categorization in capitalist economies (see, e.g., Bonacich 1972, 1979; Gordon, Edwards, and Reich 1982; Greenberg 1980; Mullings 1978; Wolf 1982). In Palermo, the late date of immigration and the near absence of working-class organization mean that the dual labor market, with its effect on the identity of immigrant workers, is still in formation.

Yet, by 1990, working Palermitans were already acutely conscious of the status divide between jobs "fit" for immigrants and those "fit" for them. My conversations in the piazza with unemployed and underemployed young men, for example, frequently turned to the difficulties of finding work. They stressed that as desperate as they were for work, they would never stoop to washing stairways in local residential buildings. Washing stairs represents for many the job of last resort, and apartment renters and owners alike in Albergheria prefer to hire out the task. According to these young men, their parents would sooner support them for years than endure the shame of a son publicly humiliating both himself and them by accepting such a lowly task.

A young man once told me how a Ghanaian had come to replace a Sicilian man from a nearby town as our building's stair cleaner. The Sicilian relentlessly pursued higher fees in exchange for sloppy work and eventually quit coming to work altogether. By contrast, the African regularly washed the steps as clean as a plate. What captivated the attention of my narrator was not the admirable work ethic of the immigrant – to take seriously such a task was actually laughable to him – but the tragedy of the Sicilian *poveretto* ("wretch") whose humiliation more than excused his poor performance.

The question of race and racism: Tunisian "Moroccans" and Moroccan "Turks"

The material deprivations suffered on the labor market and in housing and services by immigrants express and facilitate their continued marginalization in western Europe. In many cases these forces underwrite the conflation of socially significant populations as essential or quasi-biological entities. In this regard, racism acts as an ideology: a set of enduring, publicly shared beliefs regarding people's relationship with the world and social relations within it, which explain, justify, or challenge these relationships (Reeves 1983). Following Antonio Gramsci (1971), I treat ideology as part of the strategies and practices through which historically specific class coalitions attempt to consolidate hegemonic power in the face of opposition (see also Hall 1986; Saxton 1990). Ideology is more than a coherent political statement, however; it is also the contradictory "common sense" with which people approach their world. In the context of inequality, racism refers to both ideologies and practices that serve to rank and naturalize populations (Balibar 1991a). Given the nature of the research, however, I was able to gather more material on what people said about immigrants than what they did to them. Accordingly, my account in this section stresses workers' views; whenever possible I supplement these accounts with immigrants' reactions to Sicilians, and with the appraisals of concerned scholars and local observers.

This section asks whether and to what extent working Palermitans employ racial categories to describe and explain the presence of Africans and Asians, and the formation of a split job market. First, I present working people's knowledge, stereotypes, and racial categorizations of their foreign neighbors. Then I survey the extent to which they impute to these categorizations additional, undesirable qualities that make immigrants threatening and might justify exclusionary action against them.

As one would expect among people with little education living in a country with a short and distant colonial history, working Sicilians' knowledge of immigrants and their countries is meager, and their views on race vague. They tend to lump all immigrants under several Sicilian terms signifying dark skin, such as *marocchini* ("Moroccans"), *nivuri* ("blacks"), and *tuichi* ("Turks"). "Moroccan" denotes a dark-skinned foreigner, and has been used by many Sicilians since at least World War II. "Black," whether in the Sicilian form (*nivuri*) common to poor Palermo or the Italian one (*neri*) of New Palermo, is used for the same purpose, though less frequently. For the educated, *neri*, which is used to refer, for example, to blacks in the United States, has assumed some importance in the debate on racism in Italy. *Negri* ("negroes") and *tunisini* ("Tunisians") similarly denote dark-skinned foreigners.[5]

However, no term for immigrants so distinguishes working Palermitans as does the commonly heard *tuichi* ("Turks"). Indeed, mention of the term, so emblematic is it of the lively historical consciousness of old Palermo, invariably brings a smile to the faces of local scholars and other observers of life in the old city. The principal local meaning of "Turk" is dark skinned, and it is applied to appropriately colored Sicilians as well as to foreigners. When applied to Sicilians, it is used as a tease or a nickname. A family in Albergheria, for example, prodded their daughter into a rage by calling her *turca*. Or, an old man might be known as *tuichisceddu*, dark and short.

But *tuichi* connotes danger or alarm as well. Professor Vincenzo Guarrasi (personal communication) traces this usage to the days of piracy in the western Mediterranean. To this day, "*mamma li tuichi!*" ("Mom, the Turks!") commonly signifies exclamation or alarm throughout southern Italy. Or, the unfortunate Sicilian might be *pigghiatu ri tuichi*, literally imprisoned or pursued by "Turks," but also confused or taken advantage of (Rosario Lentini, personal communication). Thus, *tuichi*, when applied to Africans and Asians, denotes not only their characteristic appearance but also carries the connotation of threatening outsiders as well as insiders.

People in Albergheria and Zisa typically employ terms for immigrants, whether the common *tuichi* or the rarer *nivuri*, imprecisely and interchangeably. To a group of Sicilian men conversing in the piazza, passing Ghanaians may be *tuichi* today, *marocchini* tomorrow, and *nivuri* next week. Similarly, these Sicilians make little effort to distinguish between the various immigrant populations in a rigorous and systematic manner. It is no exaggeration to say that the same group of chatting locals that labels Ghanaians *marocchini* may well call Tunisians *tuichi* and Moroccans *nivuri*.

Working Palermitans do, of course, perceive and note broad differences in physical appearance; for example, people tell of their initial shock at seeing the blackness of the sub-Saharans. These distinctions, however, remain crude at present. The label *cinesi* ("Chinese") distinguishes Filipinos from others, and *negri* refers specifically to African-Americans and sub-Saharan Africans, while *neri* is broad enough to cover all immigrants. One interviewee illustrated the looseness of these distinctions in memorable fashion. I asked him to tell me how he would verbally distinguish a really dark man from Ghana from a light-skinned "Turk" from Tunisia. He thought for a moment, smiled, and replied: "Well, instead of saying *che tuichi* ["what a Turk"], I'd say *Madonna che tuichi!* ["Madonna, what a Turk!"]".

I attribute the characteristically vague usage of these terms to several factors. Certainly, the novelty and recent date of immigration to contemporary Sicily puts the burden of distinction on a small number of dialect terms. Furthermore, the low educational levels in poor neighborhoods mean that people there know next to nothing about countries such as Ghana, Tunisia, and Morocco. For some, these labels become conflated with nationality. One man, who had attained an elementary school education at night school and who rightly prided himself on his ample knowledge of politics, was embarrassed to learn that the Ghanaian who cleaned the stairway in his apartment building was not actually a "Moroccan."

What people do know about immigration they learn through the media, particularly television. In 1990, the year of this research, the media devoted much attention to the issues of immigration and racism, and to the debate and eventual passage of the immigration law. Working Palermitans now know, for instance, that politicians and cultural figures call the *tuichi* by names such as *immigrati di colore* or *immigrati extracomunitari* ("immigrants of color" or "immigrants from outside the European Community"). Palermitans continue to use *tuichi*, however, unless they are mocking the pretensions of the bourgeoisie or the rhetoric of politicians.

Can these imprecise, often interchangeable, and stereotypical categories employed by working people be labeled racist? Some features of popular characterizations – the habitual use of the plural form and the indiscriminant lumping together of the various nationalities, for example – resemble racist thought in that they dissolve the individual into a collectivity and erect us–them distinctions in which "their" differences are forced into a single category (Balibar 1991c; Miles 1989; Van Dijk 1987). In my estimation, however, these features have more to do with Sicilian workers' low levels of education, the novelty of immigration and diversity, and their exclusion from political life with its attention to consistent categorization.

This is not to say that the connotation of threat carried by the *tuichi*, in combination with the highly charged Italian stereotypes of Arabs as perverse and fanatical Muslims (Gallini 1989; Leschiutta 1989), and of blacks as both dangerous and glamorous (Portelli 1989), will not, in the future, furnish the vehicle for essentializing and racist categorizations of immigrants. Nevertheless, results from interviews and questionnaire surveys in Albergheria and questionnaire surveys among students at Garibaldi in Zisa show that working Palermitans rarely characterize immigrants in a manner that I would call racist, based on the definition developed at the beginning of this section. Significant in this regard are the responses to the survey questions on: (1) the importance of race; (2) race as a valid reason for restricting immigration; (3) Sicilian–immigrant intermarriage; (4) comparisons of Sicilian versus immigrant populations; (5) comparisons of different immigrant groups; and (6) the immigrants' responsibility for Palermo's problems. (See the Appendix for the complete questionnaire.)

1 At Garibaldi school in Zisa only 5 out of 54 students agreed with the statement that "A person's race is important and the white race is the best," while 49 out of 54 chose the alternative statement, "A person's race is not important." In the Albergheria sample, only 1 out of 14 voiced the former opinion while fully 13 out of 14 chose the latter.[6]

2 At Garibaldi, only 2 out of 54 would restrict immigration on the grounds that it would contaminate the white race, while 1 out of 14 similarly expressed themselves in Albergheria.

3 Regarding intermarriage between Italians and immigrants, 37 out of 54 of the Garibaldi students said they thought it is happening or will happen, 7 out of 54 objected to it, 1 out of 54 pre-empted the question by calling for repatriation, and 9 out of 54 did not respond. In Albergheria, a full 10 out of 14 thought intermarriage was happening or would happen, while 2 objected to it and 2 were indifferent. One qualified his objection to intermarriage as "not right for my sister."

4   When asked to evaluate immigrants generally in relation to Sicilians, most (35 out of 55) of the Zisa sample said they were the same, while 10 out of 55 claimed immigrants were "dirty and dangerous," and about the same proportion countered that they were "more honest and industrious" than Sicilians. In Albergheria, too, a majority (12 out of 15) described immigrants as equals, while 3 out of 15 saw them as dirty and dangerous.

5   When I asked whether and which immigrant groups were relatively better or worse, 30 out of 55 of the students at Garibaldi saw them as all similar or did not know, while 25 out of 55 agreed to differences but did not list them. In Albergheria, 7 out of 14 said immigrants were all similar, 4 out of 14 did not know, and 3 out of 14 suggested that Filipinos are good at domestic work and North Africans are good at sales.

6   The questionnaire also asked people to attribute responsibility for Palermo's unemployment and lack of industry to the following phenomena: mafia, national government, regional and city government, African and Asian immigration, and Palermitans themselves. Respondents were to put a "1" next to the most responsible phenomena, a "2" next to the second offender, and so on. In the Zisa sample, the mafia, national government, and the regional and city governments shouldered the blame, collecting 27 out of 57, 14 out of 57, and 11 out of 57 of the first place votes, respectively. Immigrants, by contrast, received but 1 first, 2 seconds, 7 thirds, 6 fourths, and 49 fifths and sixths. Albergherians, for their part, blamed the city's condition on the national government (9 out of 14), while only 1 gave immigrants anything but the lowest rating of responsibility.

In sum, the attitudes towards Africans and Asians of working people in Palermo, as expressed in interviews and questionnaires with these two samples, are far from racist. These Palermitans do not blame immigrants for the chronic problems of the city and do not vilify them in essentialist terms. This is not to say that "Turks" do not figure in the calculus of worry over jobs and security that is reckoned daily by the poor, as I describe later. It is also possible that my status as an intellectual, that is, as one perceived to be a vigilant censor of racism, may have made people cautious in their pronouncements on race and immigration. Before discussing the issue of distortion in the questionnaire results, I examine this possibility more closely.

Teun Van Dijk's (1987) study of white "talk and text" about minorities furnishes a set of analytical tools for uncovering racism beneath apparently non-racist discourse. Drawing on hundreds of interviews conducted in the Netherlands (and some in California), he demonstrates how racist discourse as propagated by elites is reproduced through everyday white "positive self-presentation" and "negative other-presentation." With regard to non-elite "talk and text," discourse analysis reveals a typically racist form and content. Immigrants and minorities, for example, tend to be portrayed as fundamentally different, hostile, and unwilling to adapt to Western ways, and as competitors unfairly advantaged by government. Van Dijk shows how this racist discourse is reproduced through storytelling, forms of argumentation, semantic moves, style, and rhetoric.

The representation of immigrants in Italy as of 1990, focusing on the issues of anti-racism and integration, is more positive than elsewhere in western Europe. Elite validation of racist stereotypes is therefore less common in Italy. Nevertheless, some working Palermitans do utilize these strategies in their positive self-presentation and negative immigrant-presentation. They regard immigrants not so much as different kinds of people, but as threats to Sicilian security because of their willingness to work for less pay and because of supposed government favoritism towards foreigners. Sicilian workers, too, are sometimes willing to contravene norms against racist talk on the basis of "true" stories. They might also employ the "empathy argument," as did a man in Albergheria who argued against immigration this way: "What do they do, these *tuichî*?," he asked rhetorically. "They suffer. Washing windshields at stoplights, selling lighters on the street – this isn't a life." His hands clapped together in supplication for his listener's understanding, he reached the logical conclusion that it would be better for the immigrants themselves if they were sent back home.

Palermitans are not strangers to rhetorical ploys such as irony and understatement. More than once I observed conversations where a speaker received a good laugh at the suggestion that "signor Martelli," the Socialist Party member who sponsored the bill on immigration, would no doubt be delighted to find several stinking "immigrants of color" living as squatters in the stairway of his Rome mansion.

On balance, however, few working Palermitans express racist ideology, whether in the overt form of questionnaire opinions on the superiority of the white race, or in the camouflaged form of discursive strategies. That only some employ these techniques of positive self-presentation and negative other-presentation does not mean that people do not worry about the effect of immigration on their lives. But working-class talk and thought about Africans and Asians generally does not seem to be conditioned by the "strategic management of delicate talk" which Van Dijk (1987) sees as symptomatic of racist discourse. Indeed, in 1990, workers were only beginning to become aware of norms against racist talk. This is seen in the rarity of semantic moves such as "apparent denial," where the speaker covers her- or himself with the protective "I'm not a racist but . . ."

There are several other reasons why I claim that the subjects of the research did not significantly modify their opinions on immigration. First, the nature of the data collection vouchsafes the results. By the time I interviewed people and gave out the questionnaire in Albergheria, I had lived there for over six months and was accepted as a legitimate researcher and not a scandal-mongering journalist. Moreover, the researchers at the Social Center, who have their fingers on the pulse of the neighborhood, confirmed my findings (Don Cosimo Scordato, Dr. Donatella Natoli, personal communication). I spoke with students in four different classes at the Zisa school, as well as with teachers, before I administered the questionnaire. Most importantly, a divergence between opinion and behavior towards immigrants would have signaled covert racism, and this I did not find to any significant degree.

Sicilians of all classes do subject immigrants to "a thousand little exploitations" such as exaggerated rents and prices, and underpayment for work (Professor Roberto Rovelli, personal communication); but many Palermitans express disgust at reports of anti-immigrant violence and politics in the north of Italy. The Social Center in Albergheria, as well as other centers and associations that deal with immigrants and the indigenous poor of the old city, report no violence or ill will in working-class Palermo. Rather, some speak of peaceful cohabitation as exemplified by intermarriage, children playing together, friendships, and the exchange of services (childcare for house cleaning, for example). On Sunday afternoons, immigrant families gather with what seems to be most of working-class Palermo at the Foro Italico – an area combining elements of a fair and amusement park that stretches along Palermo's waterfront.

Third, and finally, immigrants themselves do not speak of confronting racism in the working-class areas in which they live. While some point to exploitative employers and the stigmatizing association of domestic work and dark skin, more immigrants complain about Sicilian deficits of a different sort: ignorance about their homes, general cultural backwardness, and the lack of a work ethic. Ghanaians, Moroccans, and others told me exasperating tales of their Sicilian neighbors seriously inquiring whether such common objects as cars, houses, and watches existed in their countries (for similar accounts, see Crisantino 1992). While this ignorance does not constitute racism in a negative and openly hostile form, it may be linked to a disinterest and mythologizing of the Other. Sicilians asked me no such questions about the United States; rather, they sought to appear impressed by the modernity and power of my country.

The question of status and security: working-class understandings of immigrant employment

Given a large immigrant population and general material scarcity, it is noteworthy that most workers interviewed in Albergheria and Zisa do not avail themselves of stereotypes that might comfort them by pinning the blame for their hardships on Africans and Asians. However, there remains more to say about their reaction; for while working people do not vilify immigrants, they do worry that immigrants will threaten precarious Sicilian economic well-being. This fear finds expression in workers' evaluations of immigrant employment and comparisons of Sicilian emigration and current immigration. In each instance workers' views are profoundly ambivalent. In tracing this ambivalence to working-class experience and consciousness, I attempt to show how attention to local culture and class benefits analysis of European reactions to immigration and essentialist ideologies.

Without a doubt, the biggest working-class concern in Palermo regarding foreign workers is the threat the latter represent to the job security of the former. In interviews and discussions, and on the questionnaire, I sought Palermitans' views on immigrant work, on immigrants as both competitors and potential employees, and on the ramifications of immigration for Sicilian security and status. These understandings both recognize and minimize the insignificance of the Sicilian–foreigner competition already described.

Working Palermitans commonly characterize the jobs worked by immigrants as *i più umili*, "the most humble." These "humble" jobs read like a list of the humiliating employment once reserved for poor Sicilians and now actively rejected by them with a memory of that humiliation – washing dishes, washing stairs, temporary manual labor such as unloading goods at the markets, domestic work, and, in the countryside, shepherding, and agricultural day labor. Sicilian workers have little or no idea that some immigrants, particularly Filipino women who work as full-time domestics or caregivers for the elderly and infirm, enjoy job security, benefits, and good wages, at over $1,000 a month.

Sicilian workers correctly point out that immigrants, too, suffer the indignities of "black" work. On the one hand, employers exploit their marginality; on the other, they are constrained to work for less, which, nevertheless, may not be a drawback for someone used to Third-World wages. Yet Sicilian workers also note the intolerance towards and exploitation of immigrants. Respondents in the Zisa sample, for instance, observed that immigrants suffer humiliation as well as economic exploitation. One respondent saw racism as the cause of maltreatment. In the Albergheria sample, the majority of the respondents (9 out of 14) similarly saw foreign workers as victims of exploitation and humiliation.

Even for working-class Palermitans, immigrants are considered potential employees in addition to potential competitors. Albergherians commonly hire Africans to clean the stairways in their apartment buildings. This willingness to take on foreigners is evidenced by answers to the questionnaire inquiry: "If you were an employer, for what reason would you hire or not hire an immigrant?" At Garibaldi, a full 42 out of 50 said they would hire such a person, compared with 8 out of 50 who would not, on the grounds that Sicilians should be hired. In Albergheria, too, 12 out of 14 agreed to the hypothetical hiring (although two specified that it should occur only if a Sicilian first refused), while 2 out of 14 objected. Constituents of the two samples, however, weighed their decisions somewhat differently. In Zisa, 28 out of 50 claimed they would base hiring on the basic similarity of Sicilians and immigrants, 9 out of 50 because immigrant labor is cheaper, and 5 out of 50 because immigrants are better workers. In Albergheria, by contrast, 4 out of 14 would hire immigrants to give them work, 2 out of 14 on the basis of individual merit, 1 out of 14 because they are similar to Sicilians, and 1 out of 14 because they are cheaper.

These figures do not show what many regard as the most attractive feature of immigrant laborers, namely, their reliability. For example, the story of an owner-operator of an autobody shop stands out. He often considers hiring Tunisians but stops himself out of concern for Sicilian unemployment. A friend, also in the business, speaks glowingly of the efficiency and reliability of his skilled Tunisian workers; he pays them a fair wage (about 1.1 million lire/month or nearly $1,000 at 1990 exchange rates) but "of course" cannot afford to document them. Continuing to hire Sicilians, the owner-operator complains that they attempt to take advantage of him at every turn. In short, his moral obligation to his immoral fellow Sicilians forces him to forgo excellent foreign workers. Shaking his head at this dilemma, he commented, "I could get five of them [Tunisians] just like that and yet I deny myself. It's just not right."

Yet many working Palermitans continue to see the presence of immigrants as menacing their job security, notwithstanding their own evaluations of immigrants as reliable workers, and the recognition that foreigners are confined to low status and low pay in the dual labor market. For example, the questionnaire posed two alternative interpretations of the effects of foreigners on the labor market: (1) "They do not have a large effect because they perform jobs refused by Sicilians"; and (2) "They take work from us because they accept less." In the Zisa sample, 32 out of 54 chose the first response, while 22 out of 54 chose the second. In the Albergheria sample, 8 out of 14 chose the first, and 6 out of 14 the second.

The phrasing of this question, which forces some acknowledgment of the dual labor market, no doubt works to under-represent working Palermitans' ability simultaneously to recognize and minimize labor-market arrangements. This facility for contradictory interpretation is more pronounced in the responses to the question concerning who profits and who suffers from the undocumented employment of foreigners. Without hesitation, people in the Zisa and Albergheria samples listed themselves as well as immigrants as victims, and employers and the government as beneficiaries.

Discussions and interviews corroborate this analysis. Time and again, interviewees described the relegation of foreign workers to the lower tier of the dual labor market, as well as the Sicilians' own refusal to seek similar work. Yet they summarized the effect of immigrant employment as essentially negative: people commonly claimed that immigrants, by accepting lower wages, drove down wages for all jobs. One woman, who did not begrudge people fleeing hardship through immigration to Palermo, insisted that foreign domestic workers, or *colf,* had accounted for a precipitous decline in wages for domestic work – from 15,000 to 5,000 lire per hour (from about $12 to $4 per hour), she claimed. The claim of 15,000 lire per hour is misguided. According to staff members at API–COLF and ACLI–COLF, the two major employment agencies for domestic workers in Palermo, *colf* wages have been unaffected except for a slight and temporary decrease at the time of arrival of the first foreign workers. In 1990, both foreign and indigenous *colf* of medium qualification ("second category") received 6–7,000 lire per hour (about $5 to $6 per hour), already in excess of the national legal minimum of 4,650 lire per hour (about $4 per hour).

Another common complaint is that employers, in hiring "black" foreign labor, circumvent the national (union) contractual agreements that would otherwise serve as benchmarks for wages and benefits in Palermo. While it is true that immigrants, especially those without documentation, enjoy far less legal recourse than do Sicilians against unfair employment practices, this claim too seems far fetched. As economists and sociologists (not to mention Palermitans of all classes) well know, "black" work is rampant in Palermo. It is the circumvention and not the observation of national standards for employment that is the rule of the day, particularly at the bottom of the labor market. In short, working people in Palermo both recognize and exaggerate immigrant employment and its consequences for their fragile security. I will argue that this contradiction in their interpretation amounts to a characteristic and defining ambivalence or contradiction with regard to foreign workers.

There is a similar contradiction in Sicilian accounts of foreigners taking up residence in working-class neighborhoods. People in the Zisa and Albergheria samples unanimously decry the degradation of the old city and the shortage of decent housing. It is into condemned and substandard housing that Africans and Asians move. People from these areas often rent to immigrants, at sometimes inflated prices and with little attention to improvements or even basic maintenance. Yet some people in Albergheria also hold immigrants responsible for housing degradation (and attendant ills such as competition for housing and rising rents). At the nearby southern end of via Porta del Castro, the narrow street is darkened by beams which criss-cross it to support the buildings on either side. Some point to this obstruction and decay as an example of the "ghetto" that immigrants can create; but the damage surely antedates the inhabitation by Africans by decades.

The question of status and security: of emigrants and immigrants

A striking feature of current immigration to Sicily is that it is directed to an island which has been characterized for a century by large-scale emigration (Renda 1989). Emigration became a way of life for Sicilians from the end of the nineteenth century to the 1970s, with the exception of the Fascist period. Up until World War II, the majority of emigrants were peasants from interior areas, destined for the Americas and Australia. In the postwar period, however, Sicilians made western Europe and northern Italy their principal destinations. While emigration affected the interior agricultural provinces the most, Palermitans too know about the phenomenon; some emigrated themselves and many more know of other emigrants, particularly in recent decades. Many current residents of Palermo, moreover, came from the Sicilian interior in the postwar period. Most of the people in my sample, particularly the students at the school in Zisa, are too young to have participated in emigration, but they are familiar with emigration from the experiences of their families.

At the same time, immigration caught many Sicilians by surprise because Sicily had undergone none of the economic growth they associated with postwar migratory patterns. The increasing segmentation of the European labor market, particularly the demand for cheap and flexible labor, directs immigrants to the lower levels of all economic sectors in rich and poor regions alike. Although they do not similarly explain this unexpected turn to immigration, many Sicilians ponder the paradoxes of the transformation from emigration to immigration. For these reasons, I surveyed how working Palermitans interpret both Sicilian emigration and current African and Asian immigration, singly and in comparison. Again, I find a telling and characteristic contradiction in their accounts.

In interviews and on questionnaires, I sought understanding about the following aspects of Sicilian emigration: (1) its causes; (2) typical employment for emigrants; (3) problems particular to life in the United States; and (4) exploitation and intolerance in northern Italy. For these working-class Palermitans, it was the massive unemployment and terrible *fame,* or "hunger," that drove hundreds of thousands of Sicilians to leave in search of work. In particular, they point to the 1960s and early 1970s, when Sicilians (and other southern Italians) streamed to Switzerland, West Germany, and France, where they worked in factories, construction, mines, and services. In the industrial heartlands of northern Italy, Sicilians performed those "most humble" jobs refused by northerners. Here, at least, emigrants often landed documented employment, and their condition improved with time.

Working-class assessments of the problems and the experiences of Sicilians in the United States and northern Italy underscore broader ideas about Sicily's reputation in Italy and beyond. Respondents in the two groups express a consensus that Sicilian emigration to America was a success story. "We even brought a certain fantasy to your country," a man of sixty told me with pride. Those who did see problems for Sicilians in the United States (28 out of 46 at Garibaldi, and 4 out of 14 in Albergheria) listed only temporary impediments to adaptation, such as language difficulties and differences of culture. Few listed ethnic and racial antagonism with dominant whites, or with blacks or Puerto Ricans.[7]

Interpretations of Sicilian life in northern Italy, by contrast, are tales of exploitation, discrimination, even *razzismo.* Some 40 out of 55 students in the Garibaldi sample and 11 out of 14 people in the Albergheria sample responded "yes" to the question of whether Sicilian emigrants in the north experienced exploitation in the form of underpay and bad working conditions, but some also noted northern Italians' sense of superiority. Interviewees, moreover, dwelled on northern "racism" against Sicilians, recalling the exploitation of southern immigrants in the north and their stigmatization as *terroni* and *africani*. Donald Pitkin's (1985) moving account of a Calabrian family who emigrated to an area near Rome illustrates anti-southernism and how families remember it. It is 1938 and the father of the family, anxious about his pregnant wife, has rushed to get a doctor. The doctor is visibly disgusted by the sight of this southern woman, aged 40 and with child, living in a hut. His assessment: "You Calabrians are like Africans, like beasts" (Pitkin 1985: 45). Some interviewees specified that only a minority of northerners are racists, and that the treatment of southerners has improved with time; but most contrasted the hospitality of the south with the aloof hostility of the north.

Anti-southernism also touches on current political phrasings of the old "southern question" (Gramsci 1971). That is, political commentators have identified southern mafia, corruption, and persistent underemployment as impediments to Italian progress. No constituency in northern Italy has exploited these truths – for they do characterize large parts of the south – more successfully for political gain than the Lombard League (LL – Lega Lombarda).[8] According to followers of the League, southerners control the national government in Rome, which they use to direct northern taxes into southern pockets and to implement hiring policies which staff public agencies throughout the country with southerners. Some League supporters go so far as to claim that southerners have taken control of the northern economy and subverted the culture of their hosts. Emma Bassini suggests that southerners are responsible for low birth rates in Lombardy:

Lombard women . . . have always transmitted to their children the culture and traditions of Lombardy, based on our values of: mutual respect, honesty, hard work, altruism, etc. Presently our centralist state under southern hegemony has forced on Lombardy southern culture in which unfortunately predominate: cleverness [*furbizia*], the dominance of the strongest, arrogance, corruption and often even violence. The Lega Lombarda sees in the declining birth rate in Lombardy the uneasiness of a people that, seeing itself enslaved, has decided no longer to reproduce.[9]   *(quoted in Manconi 1990: 98)*

Working-class Palermitans take umbrage at these caricatures of lazy, scheming, mafioso southerners; mere mention of the League is enough to insure an avalanche of rebuke, counter-argument, and denial. In interviews, people described the League variously as "the ruin of Italy" (*la rovina d'Italia*), "crazy racists" (*razzisti pazzi*), and "nuts" (*gente saltata*).

They acknowledge that the party represents the minority view in the north, but give anti-southernism as the main reason why they would never move north.

Caricatures put out by the League represent only an extreme and highly publicized portrayal of the common image of a corrupt and backward south. A recent study in the northern city of Pavia demonstrated that the youth there express more antipathy towards southerners than towards any other category of "foreigner," be it blacks, Jews, Arabs, or Orientals (Colucci *et al.* (1989), Franchini and Guidi (1993: 44), and Piccoli (1993: 399) provide accounts of anti-southernism). Working-class Palermitans inevitably counter by claiming "the fish stinks from the head," that is, the "real mafia" is the national government in Rome and the financial center in Milan.

I understood the intensity of this resentment one day when I entered a small shop in Albergheria. Although I had done little business there, the man took me into his confidence as soon as he learned I was an American. He proceeded to harangue me on the subject of the "Roman" exploitation of Sicily. The politicians in Rome, he said, stay awake at night concocting new taxes on small, family businesses like his. The latest fiscal imposition was a tax, yes, on floor space. Orlando, the mayor of Palermo, had been ousted because he had challenged this corruption: "They're like a gang of thieves, who kill the only honest member." In short, the "Romans" who disrespectfully call Sicilians *terroni* think only of their pocketbooks. The real tragedy, he concluded, was that Sicily could have been an American state, if only the "Romans" had not talked Roosevelt out of supporting the Sicilian movement for American statehood after World War II. At this point his son came in. The man shook his head: "And to think he could have been an American. But he's an Italian, unfortunately!" He nearly spat on the newly taxed floor.

Working Palermitans' views of current immigration resemble in many ways their accounts of Sicilian emigration. According to them, Africans and Asians are fleeing poverty and oppression, perform tasks refused by self-respecting locals, and suffer exploitation, indifference, and even intolerance. These Sicilians are conversant with the travails of migration and empathize with immigrants who must leave family and country behind to take a step forward. One man described immigration this way: "By now, the world is like a village; you search for work [everywhere] just to live, to support your family." Some carry the parallel further, noting the discrimination faced by both groups. Another told me in a matter-of-fact tone that just as northern Italians thought themselves superior to southern emigrants, so too do Sicilians consider themselves above Africans and Asians (for a similar appraisal from south-west Sicily, see Cusumano 1976).

Public officials and the representatives of relevant institutions have made explicit this implicit comparison or equation between emigration and immigration. While talk about the duties of a "country of emigration" is also heard at the national level, nowhere is this idiom more resonant than in Sicily. Almost all the institutional representatives whom I interviewed in Palermo (and elsewhere on the island) derived from their analysis of the experience of Sicilian emigration a sense of obligation for contemporary Sicilians to receive and respect immigrants. Some pointed to the "historical memory" of emigration as the cause for Sicilian tolerance towards foreigners. Others lamented the lapse of such memories and widespread indifference if not intolerance towards immigrants; but all agreed that the duty remained and that Sicilians, especially the working classes, who are thought most susceptible to intolerance, must be taught this if they do not already know it. Reflecting this stance, the Social Center in Albergheria and the equivalency courses at Garibaldi in Zisa both alert residents to the dangers of intolerance and promote the idea that former emigrants owe understanding and sympathy to new immigrants.

For working Palermitans, however, the basic economic similarities of the two migrations do not so easily translate into an obvious duty towards, or an identification of common cause with, immigrants. There are those who, like a tradesman from Albergheria, say that Sicily is "their America," their land of opportunity. Immigrants, he said, have as much right to come to Sicily as his own forefathers had to go to the United States. According to volunteers at Caritàs, the charitable organ of the Catholic Church, the indigenous poor often observe that immigration has not changed their lives: "we had nothing before and we have nothing now." But most workers are profoundly ambivalent if and when they compare emigration and immigration; for just as their interpretation of foreign participation on the labor market is riven by contradiction and tension, so too is their interpretation of emigration and immigration. Both engage more general class anxieties and insecurities. Thus empathy for the immigrant's lot, and understanding of the mechanisms of common oppression, are checked by a refusal to identify with Third-World immigrant populations considered inferior, or at least undeserving of opportunity in Italy.

Responses to four interview and questionnaire topics eliciting comparisons of the two migrations illustrate this characteristically ambivalent working-class position.

1 The first asked whether immigrants will contribute in the future to Italian development through their labor and culture or whether they will instead take resources away from Italians. In the Zisa sample, a slim majority saw immigrants (27 out of 51) contributing, while support in Albergheria was higher (8.5 out of 12).

2 The second question presented three choices: (1) supporting regulated immigration because 27 million Italians emigrated abroad for work in this century; (2) not supporting it because of fears of contaminating the white race; or (3) not supporting it because of joblessness among Italians. Again, a slim majority supported immigration (31 out of 55 at Garibaldi, and 7.5 out of 14 in Albergheria), and a sizable minority objected on the grounds of unemployment.

3 The third question asked whether the national government, in passing Law #39, was irresponsible with regard to Italians in the sense that it permits immigration, which in turn endangers Italian jobs, wages, and security. Many supported the government's action: 22 out of 51 in Zisa, and 4.5 out of 11 in Albergheria. These results should be treated with caution, however. As I found out in classroom discussions in Zisa, few actually know what the law entails, despite the heavy media coverage of the prolonged and heated parliamentary debate at the time. In fact, 14 out of 51 students at Garibaldi and 4 out of 11 people in the Albergheria sample answered "don't know" to the question, and many others responded with a simple "yes" or "no."

Popular outrage over an immigrant protest held in the spring of 1990 also demonstrated a lack of working-class support for measures protecting immigrants. The "strike of the immigrants," as it was known in Albergheria, was actually entitled *La Solidarietà e i diritti non hanno colore* ("Solidarity and Rights Have No Color"). Organized by the union CGIL (Confederazione Generale Italiana del Lavoro), the brief march protested against poor immigrant living and working conditions (*Giornale di Sicilia*, 16 November 1990). Many Albergherians interpreted the action as a brazen and selfish claim by immigrants on the resources due but so long denied to average Palermitans. They also criticized the union for, in effect, dismissing their own grievances by giving priority to immigrants. Even those sympathetic to the march lamented the tactical blunder committed by CGIL officials in separating the protest of foreign and indigenous workers. The march stirred a brief controversy that did not lead to any political response on the part of local workers. Their reaction was not lost on union officials, however. Within months, the CGIL had scheduled a new protest in which both foreign and Sicilian workers united in their call for better opportunities.

4   The fourth question asked whether, and how, Sicilian emigration is comparable with current immigration to Sicily. Here, many saw more difference than similarity in the two migrations: 26 out of 49 (with 10 "don't knows") in Zisa, and 7 out of 13 in Albergheria. I had anticipated as points of comparison the cultural and racial makeup of the populations, and the economic and political circumstances of their migrations. Many respondents, especially in the Zisa sample, limited themselves to one-word answers. The respondents who did elaborate distinguished between the two population movements in terms of time period, economic development in the host countries (Sicilian emigrants worked in factories, whereas immigrants work on the street and in the fields), and motivation (today's immigrants have left their home countries for reasons of political freedom, whereas Sicilians left in search of work). Several respondents also claimed that "immigrants do not work as hard as we do" and that "we're just different."

These questionnaire results could be seen simply as evidence of divided opinion. However, I argue that they are the numerical expression of a deeper ambivalence towards immigration, an ambivalence rooted in the precariousness of working-class life itself. Ambivalence is, in fact, a defining feature of working-class interpretation of immigration, and sets it off from the consistently pro-immigrant views of the bourgeoisie, which I describe in the following chapter.

The strength of the contradiction was impressed on me repeatedly in interviews and classroom discussions. These Sicilians acknowledge the poverty that compelled Sicilian emigration, as well as the emigrants' experience of discrimination and humiliation; and they burn with resentment at northern Italian stereotypes of the lazy and mafioso southerner. They can also discuss the motives and experiences of immigrants in terms remarkably similar to those used to describe Sicilian emigrant experiences. Furthermore, they understand their own and immigrants' exploitation to be based on the system of undocumented and underpaid labor. However, they rarely volunteer comparisons of emigration and immigration; and when asked about the comparison, more often than not they strive to deny any significant similarity in oppression and identity.

When teachers at the Garibaldi school sponsored a conference in spring 1990 on immigration, teachers of the "150 Hours Course" asked students who had emigrated to West Germany in the 1960s and 1970s to come forward and tell the audience about their experiences. Only one came forward, although several had been solicited before the conference and the entire class was required to attend. The teacher who organized the conference interpreted this reluctance as embarrassment to admit publicly to having suffered hardship (Angela Aiola, personal communication). She went on to say that it is not uncommon for students with low-paying, undocumented work to insist that they "are doing fine" (*sto bene io*) when asked about their situation. Similarly, a study found that southern Italian middle- and high-school students both recognize their marginality as southerners, and distinguish themselves as modern westerners from the Third-World immigrants in their areas (Cammarota 1989).

More than one informant was reduced to hemming and hawing at the point in the interview when I asked if the two population movements (which had already been discussed separately) were not really basically similar phenomena. When I asked one young man to compare emigration and immigration, he threw up his hands in exasperation and turned to a co-worker, pleading "what am I going to say to that?" Interviewees rehearsed all manner of potentially differentiating features, citing differences in historical period, language, and dress that skirted the question of basic similarity. After countless hesitations and revisions, most hit on this crucial distinction: Sicilians brought skills to their new countries and contributed to their development, while Africans and Asians come from lands without resources, "without history" even, and consequently lack skills and cannot contribute to Italy.

On the form and distribution of working-class views
Throughout this chapter, I have spoken in broad terms of working-class self-assessments and opinions on immigration. Now I turn to the question of the form and distribution of these views. Form, in this context, refers to logical consistency, vocabulary, and tone of opinion. It merits analysis because, as I will show in the next chapter, it diverges according to class. Examination of the distribution of opinion across the parameters of age, sex, education, and employment status permits comparison with samples drawn from opinion polls elsewhere. Also, it is important to examine the racist inclinations of young working-class Palermitans, because most of

the anti-immigrant violence and graffiti in the north of Italy has been committed by young men professing neo-nazi, neo-fascist, skinhead, and *ultra* (soccer fan of the hooligan variety) credos.

The most striking features of popular talk in Palermo are the use of dialect and logical inconsistency. I have already described the usage of various terms in Sicilian for foreigners such as *tuichi* and *marocchini*. Glaring inconsistencies abound in individual questionnaire responses, interviews, and informal discussions. For example, those who claim the superiority of the white race on the questionnaire also hold intermarriage to be acceptable and are disposed to hire immigrants on the grounds of equality. There was the local craftsman who on one occasion proposed that medals be issued to all inter-racial couples as a reward for championing equality over racism. But the next day he entertained a small crowd outside his shop with a modest proposal for ridding the island of these unwanted "Turks" who plague Palermitans at every stop-light selling cigarette lighters and washing windshields. Sicilians should take them all to the ferry, have them clean every window to a high shine, and ship them back to Tunisia, or dump them at sea, he proposed.

Low educational levels and exclusion from influential public discourse account for this characteristic inconsistency. The majority of older adults in working-class Palermo hold an elementary school qualification, and the majority of youth an eighth-grade diploma (i.e. third year of secondary school level). While meager schooling explains some of the typical lack of concern for logical consistency, the exclusion of working people from the resources, rules, and standards of influential public discourse is at least as important. Frank Reeves' (1983: 78) distinction between "specialized political discourse" and "general discourse," although formulated to distinguish between political and everyday usage, provides a useful contrast for class-specific discourse on immigration in Palermo. Politicians, institutional representatives, intellectuals, and the bourgeoisie employ a specialized discourse which is integrated, consistent, and linked to explicit ideologies. Everyday discourse, as exemplified by the Albergheria and Zisa samples, is "weakly structured," less concerned with consistency, and often made up of "unrelated explanations." While the former seeks to persuade, explain, and justify, the latter serves to express opinions. Differential access to the means and content of public and political communication tends to reinforce the general features of these discourses. With little training in and limited access to influential discourse, working Palermitans have little call to arrange their opinions in a systematic fashion.

The Palermo evidence corroborates research conducted elsewhere in Italy and Europe (see, for example, Amodio 1989; Bonifazi and Golini 1989; Guala 1989; Italia-razzismo 1990; Van Dijk 1987: 357–8). Women, youth, and, anticipating the bourgeois samples of the next chapter, more educated and higher status employees all tend to profess more tolerance for foreigners, according to these earlier studies. My results are similar, although rough indicators of class, education and job status are generally more determinant than sex and age. Union and political-party membership seem to have almost no correlation with interpretations of immigration. This is probably because working Palermitans are rarely politicized, and because neither parties nor unions in Palermo have seriously addressed the issue.

It is true that my survey data from Albergheria and Zisa do not lend themselves to an exacting measurement of the correlation between parameters and opinions: the former sample is too small, while the latter is weighted to younger people of similar education. In my estimation, however, the general working-class interpretation of immigration, which I have characterized as ambivalent and inconsistent, pessimistic but empathetic, describes the stance of most working Palermitans. There are, I think, three partial exceptions. The truly dispossessed – those who practice *l'arte di arrangiarsi* as scavengers or run illegal daily lotteries, some youth with relatively high levels of education but no acceptable job prospects, as well as those who sell goods at weekly markets or on the street – all tend to express somewhat harsher views on immigration. The grumblings of people in these categories are, nevertheless, still of a different sort from the organized animosity and outright violence facing immigrants in the Italian north, as I explore in more detail later.

Finally, working-class interpretation is more flexible and open to change than I have perhaps allowed in my description. Immigration to contemporary Sicily is a novelty, and the composition of the immigrant population is in flux as new people arrive and others move northward in search of steady work. Sicilians, unlike northern Italians, have no experience of interacting with and stereotyping incoming, subordinate populations. By not addressing immigration as an important issue, political parties have not encouraged the crystalization of views around a limited number of explicit positions characteristic of specialized political discourse.

The arrival of a Moroccan family into my building showed me the flexibility of local ideas about foreigners. The Sicilians coolly, even disdainfully, received these people, the first "Turks" to settle in this part of

Albergheria. However, the initial haughtiness was counterbalanced by curiosity and confusion. The newcomers were Moroccan yet "didn't look it," with their light skin and casual European appearance. They were from the Third World yet came from Belgium, played loud rock music, possessed championship judo skills, spoke a variety of languages, and treated everyone as equals. They spoke with pride of their Islamic faith, but the women did not veil themselves and the men did not abstain from wine or beer. The spectacle of Mohammed running sprints and performing exercises on the piazza below dumbfounded whole balconies of silent and observant Sicilian neighbors unaccustomed to such athletic displays. Within a week, the local youth were impressed by, and perhaps envious of, the Moroccans' skills, aplomb, and knowledge of the world. They would look with curiosity at the son and me as we spoke in English of the NBA (the National Basketball Association in the USA), as he told ridiculous jokes in French or complained about the ignorance of his neighbors. The entry of the Moroccan family did not dispel all the anti-immigrant prejudices of local residents, as the perception of them as exceptional suggests, but their presence did change the opinions of some. By means of exchanges of food, hospitality, and conversation with Sicilian neighbors, and through the employment of the youngest daughter in a local shop, the Moroccans were in time brought into the fabric of neighborhood life.

Interpreting the ambivalence of working Palermitans towards immigrants
This chapter has asked whether, and how, working Palermitans express "working-class racism" against Third-World immigrants. In my estimation, very few do. Few identify immigrants as a specific racial group with unalterable and undesirable qualities that constitute a threat to Sicilians and justify action against them. Rather, most express a profound ambivalence, balancing comprehension and nagging worry, expressed in the idioms of competition and threat. As longtime emigrants, Sicilians understand the pain and humiliation of immigration. They see immigrants, like themselves, as oppressed and struggling beyond decency simply to support their families. They see them performing jobs they have rejected, and even as reliable and cheap workers. At the same time, working Palermitans portray Africans and Asians as competitors on the labor market (and, to a lesser extent, for housing). They also balk at acknowledging similarities in circumstance, oppression, and identity between Sicilian emigration and current immigration. In contrast to the abstract and universalistic interpretations of immigration among Palermo's bourgeoisie and the relevant

institutions and associations, working-class views are typically informed by local language and understandings, and are stubbornly pessimistic.

In this section, I shall explore the key issue of ambivalence or ideological contradiction, which I regard as the most noteworthy finding of this study. Low levels of education, predominance of dialect over Italian, and exclusion from influential public discourse – all these hallmarks of Palermo *popolare* account, perhaps predictably, for the individual inconsistency and local color of interpretations. However, ambivalence and contradiction become characteristic and powerful because they engage fundamental class insecurities and identities. The insecurity that burdens working Palermitans stems from the precariousness of employment and a thoroughgoing marginality. While working Palermitans vehemently reject their oppression and the oppressors, they also tacitly accept their own denigration, which is argued so persuasively, so to speak, by their evident subordination.

It is precisely these understandings of self which structure the characteristic ambivalence towards foreign workers of the Sicilians I encountered. The ambivalence is pronounced, as I have shown, on the issue of immigrant participation in the labor market. People in Zisa and Albergheria can readily enumerate the lowly jobs relegated to immigrants, jobs they flatly reject, such as dishwashing and live-in domestic work. Some find that the foreigners perform these tasks more cheaply and, in particular, more reliably than fellow Sicilians. Finally, they recognize that the exploitation of Africans and Asians, through underpayment and lack of documentation, for example, is only an exaggerated form of their own exploitation. Yet, in the face of such acknowledgments, many workers steadfastly maintain that immigrants "take their bread," that immigration would be fine "if only there were work for us." The logic behind such thinking seems to be: we are unemployed, they work, therefore they take our work; and, foreigners should not enjoy the opportunity to work in our country, even if we refuse the jobs they take, because they are undeserving in the sense that they have not contributed to it as we have. The Sicilians who pursue this logic further claim that immigrants lower wages generally, and provide employers with cheap and undocumented labor instead of the otherwise standard union-rate, documented labor. However, immigrants depress wages (if, in fact, they do) only in specific sectors, and documented work and union wages are not the rule of the day in Palermo, as local people know all too well.

The strong opinions of a young Albergherian illustrate the depth of this contradiction. At the time of the interview, he was finishing a three-month *cantiere* program for unemployed youth, after which he would perform his obligatory military service. He spoke with the detachment of someone who would confront the problem of landing work only in the distant future. When I asked him about "black" work in Palermo, he sighed, and told me the story of a friend by way of example. The friend, who possesses a trade-school degree in accounting, works full-time for the pitiful sum of 300,000 lire/month (about $250 at 1990 exchange rates). The interviewee blamed employers' cutting costs for the pervasive underemployment and undocumented employment, and also felt that the mafia gained through the clientelistic distribution of jobs and favors. He assured me that he would never accept such exploitation; nor would he humiliate himself by washing stairs like the "Turks." He elaborated on immigrant work, saying that whereas Sicilians refuse it or do it poorly, foreigners do it well. In fact, it was no longer possible to find a Sicilian to wash the stairs in his building. Later in the interview he addressed the question of immigration again. He objected to the immigrants' presence because they "steal" work from locals, and explained that employers hire them for less rather than hiring Sicilians at fair and union wages. His harsh conclusion: "They're infecting the city, we must ship them back home." When I reminded him that his friend, who, like so many, endures no African or Asian competition at his place of work, also works "black" for little, he stumbled over his words, flustered that I had made explicit the implicit contradiction in his account. He eventually proposed this resolution: his friend does not actually work very hard and, furthermore, his employer has two other workers on the payroll and so understandably cannot afford to pay higher wages.

This interview exposes the depth of working-class feeling about foreign workers on the labor market. Here is the unproblematic, if contradictory, accommodation in the popular mind of both recognition and denial of the dual labor market. Supporting this is the complex understanding of the place of working people in the system. This young man sees his class unjustly exploited by employers and the mafia; yet he also sees himself as above the detestable "Turks," whose performance of lowly tasks is both an enactment and proof of their inferiority. At the same time, the immigrant presence constitutes a threat to jobs and to the city itself. The immigrant threat is thus another manifestation of an unjust system, since it was the Italian state that aided and abetted immigration, and employers and the mafia who profit from it.

Working people's ambivalence towards immigrants also shows up in their comparison of emigration and immigration; contradictory recognition and denial structure this sense of a parallel between the two population movements. Sicilian empathy for immigrants is born of the protracted pain of Sicilian emigration and, perhaps, the related experience in the north as stigmatized *terroni*. Working Palermitans describe emigration and immigration in remarkably similar terms; yet many steadfastly deny any significant similarity between the two movements and all that the parallel entails. For example, they fail to see that Sicilians once appeared as destitute and inferior as "Africans" and "Turks" now do, that immigrants will contribute to Sicily just as Sicilians contributed to New York and Turin, that similarities in oppression and circumstance constitute some form of common identity, and require, perhaps, a responsible acceptance of immigrants and laws for their protection.

Just as the young man stumbled over the contradiction, once made apparent, in his interpretation of foreign workers on the labor market, so too did interviewees often hesitate, and grow cautious, when I asked them to make explicit their implicit comparison between themselves and the immigrants. Unfailingly, they sought to resolve this contradiction by positing differences in performance and merit. Whereas Sicilians had contributed to their new homes through their skills and labor, "Turks" bring nothing but empty bellies and untrained minds, and could never contribute to Palermo and Italy. These Sicilians push this resolution because to equate themselves with Africans and Asians would be tantamount to equating themselves, their identity and self-worth, with the absolute standard of misery that is, for them, the Third World. That immigrants are, on average, as well educated as Sicilians underscores the irony of these claims, but it does not expose those who made them as hypocritical because working Palermitans know next to nothing about the socioeconomic characteristics of the immigrant population. This solution to the status dilemma, exacerbated by the immigrant presence, also permits working Palermitans to elide their evident subordination within the national political economy. This victory is temporary at best, however, for they become associated with immigrants not simply out of general parallels between emigration and immigration, but also from living and (perhaps increasingly) working together.

The dilemma over self-worth and status explains the reluctance of many working Palermitans to see immigrants as contributors to Sicily. The following example illustrates the complexity of this position. In response to my question about the potential contribution of immigrants, a young man responded by pointing to the dangers of immigration as exemplified by the experience of the United States. What is happening there is just terrible, he exclaimed: "The Chinese mafia is now stronger than the Sicilian one!" This utterance, delivered without a hint of irony, betrays the curious workings of anti-southernism in the south. Here, the speaker stigmatizes immigrants while unwittingly accepting the unflattering stereotype of the mafioso southerner. This slip recalls the not uncommon Palermitan rejection of North Africans on the grounds that "they're too much like us" – that is, lazy, scheming, and untrustworthy.[10] I return to the notion of self-hatred later.

The nationalist element in working-class objections to immigration also explains the popular outrage over the "strike of the immigrants" described earlier. Sicilians were angered, of course, by the temerity of foreigners' demanding what they feel themselves to be owed but have long been denied by a hostile and inefficient system. What they may have feared in this incident was less the immigrants' call for decent conditions – which Sicilian emigrants abroad had also demanded – than the prospect that the government would neglect them in order to aid these "immigrants of color." For, just as Rome was thought to have permitted immigration to the detriment of the native working classes, so too could the government not be trusted to vouchsafe the rights of citizens above those of foreigners. In other words, working-class interpretations of the system anticipate the plausibility of government favoritism towards immigrants.[11]

Conclusions

As I have suggested, the question of a specifically working-class reaction to immigrants has nagged at scholars of postwar European migration. At first glance, the profound ambivalence of working Palermitans would seem wholly of a different order from the "working-class racism" of English workers documented by Annie Phizacklea and Robert Miles (1979, 1980). Yet I argue that the views of these Sicilians relate to most of the key issues in working-class interpretations of foreign labor, namely the ideological portrayal of threat (as opposed to actual competition), the dynamics of working-class insecurity, the designation of foreigners as "inferior" or "undeserving," the centrality of the state, and the structural underpinnings of ambivalence and racism.

Analysis of the dual labor market in Palermo shows little competition between foreigners and Sicilians, yet local workers represent immigrants as threatening to job security, and as cheap and reliable workers of lowly jobs. As elsewhere in Europe (and the United States), working people tend to represent foreign workers as threatening because their presence engages general class insecurities and status anxieties. In other words, it is the idea more than the reality of competition that flourishes in rich California or northern Italy, as well as in poor Sicily or the depressed parts of England.

As Etienne Balibar has keenly observed:

To the extent, however, that they [workers] project on to foreigners their fears and resentments, despair and defiance, it is not only that they are *fighting competition*; in addition, and much more profoundly, they are trying to escape their own exploitation. It is their hatred of *themselves*, as proletarians – in so far as they are in danger of being drawn back into the mill of proletarianization – that they are showing.   (*Balibar 1991e: 214*)

Balibar is writing with the experience of industrial Europe in mind. There, the flight of capital, industrial reorganization, and the deskilling of some jobs, as well as the increasing call for flexible and temporary labor, pose real threats to the security of the traditional and often unionized working class. In Palermo it is not the fear of losing the security of industrial employment that never was that fuels this self-hatred and fear of immigrants, but rather the exposure of working-class marginality. Significantly, the comprehension of immigrants shown by working Palermitans has checked the transformation of this self-hatred into the sort of xenophobic and racist rejection of immigrants that Balibar finds in France. My claim is only that in both the French and the Palermo cases class anxiety and insecurity sharpen this double-sided fear.

Several aspects of this dynamic of self- and Other-hatred bear elaboration. First, it is clear that the by now familiar forms of worker complaints about foreign workers in Europe – that immigrants receive privileged treatment from governments, undercut wages, and take work – turn as much on questions of self-worth and self-definition as on the actions of government and employers. In this portrayal of threat, European workers often counterpoise themselves as citizens, as contributors to the nation, and as bearers of labor's banner to the masses from the Third World, who are seen as undeserving of the largesse of welfare states, if not as patently inferior. It is to this dynamic that racism can bring its special efficacy.

As an ideology which defines and stigmatizes populations, racism provides a compelling explanation for whatever ails a nation or a class, and shores up native working-class status. As Stuart Hall has suggested, through racism portions of the working class can "live" out their relations to other class factions and thereby to capital itself (Hall 1980: 34). In his interpretation of English working-class racism towards blacks from the colonies, Frank Reeves observes that the "white metropolitan proletariat actually saw itself as an 'aristocracy of labor' in relation to the inferior black people of the colonies" (Reeves 1983: 55). For whites to live and work alongside blacks, then, calls into question putative white superiority. But these English workers are expressing more than just the pinch of competition or the status dilemma occasioned by the fall of empire. Reeves draws on Richard Sennet and Jonathon Cobb's (1977) *The Hidden Injuries of Class* to locate the themes of sacrifice and contribution in white discourse. The proximity of blacks in economic, residential, and status terms in effect undermines the virtue of white working-class sacrifice. By belittling black success as "unfair" and government aided, English workers thereby assert the validity of their own sacrifice, which once evoked a blue-collar "aristocracy" but whose status is now imperiled.

Working Palermitans, for their part, do not "live" out their insecurity by vilifying immigrants or supporting political enterpreneurs sensitive to the fears of local poor. However, they do often claim superiority over Africans and Asians by asserting the inferiority of the Third World, and the consequent improbability that immigrants can contribute to Sicily as Sicilian emigrants did in New York. In so doing, they draw on the general western stigmatization of the non-west. In this sense, the recurrent distinctions drawn in Europe between "north" and "south," "First" and "Third" Worlds, immigrants and nationals, are recastings of the old division of humanity into the hierarchical dichotomy of "hot" and "cold," progressive and stagnant societies (Balibar 1991a). This representation, like the racial hierarchies cast in the colonial era, remains firmly grounded in social relations, but is sufficiently flexible to offer explanatory categories for changing and complex circumstances.

Second, workers habitually represent their objections to immigrants in terms of national identity. Governments are seen as betraying workers who have contributed to the nation while unfairly privileging foreigners. Thus the slogans of the new racism in Europe sound the call to uphold the supposedly challenged rights of nationals. The National Front in Britain has warned that the British are becoming "second-class citizens" in their own country, while across the channel Le Pen cries "France for the French." The typical "co-determination" or articulation of the ideologies of nationalism and racism creates a heady political rhetoric that is able to draw on cross-class support and shield itself from criticisms of racism (Balibar 1991a, 1991b; Miles 1989). Workers in Palermo, as elsewhere, sympathize with immigrants, but also suspect that the government harms Italian nationals by assisting immigrants through legal protections and programs.

At the deepest level, the fundamentally contradictory nature of worker identity in capitalist democracies structures interpretation of foreign workers, whether blatantly racist or ambivalent. Workers, more than any other class, are both free economic participants and subordinates, whose lesser merit is manifested in their relative powerlessness to consume (Wolf

1982: 389–90). They are also both free citizens and political subordinates. Workers may therefore align themselves against capital, demanding more wages and different definitions of merit, or compete among themselves for jobs and status, either within sectors of a segmented labor market or across them. While all these options operate simultaneously, the realities and idioms of competition predominate within the working class. This is why the idioms of solidarity in Sicily are contradicted and in some cases overwhelmed by representations of threat and competition.

In some circumstances, the structures and idioms of worker solidarity, such as unions and class consciousness, can serve to counterbalance the more common representation of foreign workers as a threat. For working Palermitans, there are other elements in the balancing act of sympathy and distrust that distinguish their views of foreign workers. Understanding of popular marginality, experience of stigmatization by northerners as *terroni* and "Africans," and empathy for immigrants – rather than union-sponsored ideologies of worker internationalism – explain tolerance in their case. However, the contradictions of southern identity as experienced by poor Sicilians complicate their views of immigrants, for while some Sicilians reject intolerance towards immigrants by rejecting their own stigmatization, others disparage immigrants in the same way that northerners disparage them. In an essentially negative synthesis of self- and Other-presentation, they may reject foreigners as unwanted and inferior because they are "too much like us." In this case, working Palermitans' rejection of foreigners differs fundamentally from northerners' rejection of southerners in that the workers' pejorative assessment of foreigners is a projection of their own insecure self-image.

While the tolerance of working Palermitans may be exceptional or temporary, I suggest that a closer look at European workers' assessments of foreign workers would expose similar patterns of ambivalence obscured beneath blanket claims of "working-class racism."

3

The view from the top: bourgeois views of immigrants in Palermo

The question of bourgeois racism

In this chapter I again address the question of class variation with regard to European reactions to immigrants, this time by discussing bourgeois interactions with and interpretations of African and Asian immigrants in Palermo. This contrast with working-class views: (1) permits a disaggregation of public attitudes otherwise seen as homogeneous; (2) points to the class bases of divergent views and actions; and (3) reveals different capacities for public discourse and political action. The findings show, in fact, highly contrastive and class-specific views on immigration, racism, and anti-racism. Against the often inconsistent, locally informed, ambivalent, and stubbornly pessimistic working-class views, bourgeois Palermitans espouse a sophisticated pro-immigrant, anti-racist position, grounded in universalist ideologies.

I explain these divergent views on immigration with reference to broad differences in class experience and consciousness. Tenuous security and class self-hatred on the one hand, and empathy born of shared poverty and emigration on the other, structure working-class ambivalence. By contrast, the unhesitating enthusiasm of the bourgeois high-school and university students for paradigms favorable to immigrant rights and recognition stems from the equanimity born of a relatively secure class position, knowledge of generally accepted views on race transmitted through higher education, membership of self-styled progressive circles in a national political culture dominated by the rhetoric of anti-racism, and aspects of local culture and history deemed pertinent to these paradigms. As regards the form of these divergent views, little education and the lack of access to influential public discourse undermine the consistency of working people's opinions. Among the high-school and university students, by contrast, higher education, familiarity with paradigmatic interpretations of immigration, in particular, and political discourse, in general, all contribute to the consistency and sophistication of expression.

Yet the bourgeois position is beset by its own contradictions and inconsistencies. This becomes clear as I broaden my unit of analysis from the student samples to the bourgeoisie in general, drawing on impressions based on friendships and acquaintances among professionals, and as I introduce other evidence from Italian politics, popular culture, and the local market for domestic labor. By enlarging the framework of analysis, I reveal several telling inconsistencies in the bourgeois position on race and immigration. Of course, the lethargy of Italian politics – with which this class is associated – results in the abandonment of most initiatives favorable to immigrants. Also at issue is a dogmatic anti-racism which stifles debate on the modalities of Italian reactions to immigrants. Americans who have lived and studied in Italy over past decades note how many Italian intellectual friends have suddenly dropped the habit of criticizing race relations in the United States as Italian reactions to immigrants have come under scrutiny. In the meanwhile, however, Italian self-satisfaction cannot but have influenced general bourgeois opinion, particularly in Palermo, where Sicilian history furnishes attractive models and explanations for what is viewed as Sicilian tolerance.

A number of racial stereotypes from Italian popular culture also contradict bourgeois ideologies of anti-racism. In Palermo, ideas about the relative aptitudes of various immigrant groups arise in the power-laden interaction of stereotype and labor market. Paradoxically, Palermitans who live and work with, even hire, "Turks" check their identification with them through their claims of Sicilian superiority, while those who seek the distinction of being served by foreign *colf* proclaim the benefits of a multiracial Italy.

The contradictory bourgeois interpretation of immigrants in Palermo, then, pits tolerance and anti-racist ideology against stereotypes honed in relations of dominance, as in the labor market for domestic workers. Writers concerned with white racism concentrate on institutional racism as an expression of fundamental racial inequality, or on working-class racism as a manifestation of workers' powerlessness and labor-market segmentation. Seldom do they address bourgeois attitudes to race. No doubt this neglect reflects the tolerance of the bourgeois class as expressed in opinion polls. The few who do address it, such as Van Dijk, read this tolerance as a rhetorical façade behind which this class (particularly members of the media and the political elite) perpetuate the racial antagonism and domination which shores up white western power (Van Dijk 1987: 360–1). This characterization, although occasionally accurate, endows the bourgeois class with unrealistic intention, unity, and cynicism; its functionalism conflates effect with cause, and fails to account for the strength of ideologies of anti-racism in Italy. Perhaps it would be more accurate to say, following Immanuel Wallerstein (1991), that there exists under capitalism an enduring ideological contradiction between "universalism" and "racism." Universalist ideologies of equality and meritocracy accompany and feed the homogenizing process of commodification, while the ranking and naturalizing of large parts of the workforce permit their reproduction and exploitation.

I suggest that the explanation for contradictory bourgeois attitudes and behaviors lies in class experience and consciousness, broadly conceived. The relationship of this class to workers, foreign and national, is one of dominance, legitimated and celebrated by the ideology of capitalism. Explicit racist ideology could conceivably justify the exploitation of foreign workers, but its adoption by the bourgeoisie is untenable, given the efficacy of capitalist thought and the infamy currently attached to racism. On the other hand, the racial and ethnic categorization of immigrant labor does provide what Wallerstein calls a "non-meritocratic basis" for inequality. This is why members of the Palermo bourgeoisie regard immigrant participation in the labor market with an equanimity that contrasts with working-class emotion. Immigrants provide the bourgeois class with reliable, even fashionable, household staff; in effect, they form but another, if novel, segment of the working class, whose subordination and demerit underline bourgeois dominance and merit. Thus, bourgeois worries about immigration are confined to the issue of regulating the flow of immigrants into the country and the labor market. While working Palermitans fear their state will abandon them to receive and care for foreigners, the bourgeoisie calmly receive a dependable workforce.

Research population and research methods

I complemented investigation of "working-class racism" with two questionnaire surveys, the first in a prestigious public, classical high school (*liceo classico*), the second at the University of Palermo. Because I administered the questionnaire towards the end of my study, I was unable to devote much attention to these schools. Starting in the section "Of emigrants and immigrants," I have tried to supplement the student samples by drawing on a snowball sample consisting of the many professional people whom I met in Palermo in the course of my study (see pp. 83–99).

In terms of class structure, the high-school group represents the *alta borghesia,* or bourgeoisie proper, of New Palermo, while the university students represent both the petty bourgeoisie and the upwardly mobile working class of the countryside. Despite the noteworthy differences in the two samples – the first comprised the children of Palermo's upper professional and bureaucratic ranks, the second a broad sampling from the countryside – I treat the two together here, supported by the similarity of responses. I will argue later that this convergence of opinion stems from participation in higher education, which imparts that repertoire of attitudes that, here as elsewhere, constitutes a large component of the "cultural capital" (Bourdieu 1984) that distinguishes the lettered from the unlettered.

The first group consists of the responses of 44 students at the classical high school, which I shall call "Ruggero II." These 10 males and 34 females between the ages of 16 and 18 are in their final two years of high school. The questionnaire was administered by their philosophy teacher, whom I met through a mutual friend.

The class position of the high-school students, their experiences with and interpretations of immigrants, are wholly opposed to those of the Albergheria and Zisa samples. These students come from affluent neighborhoods in New Palermo such as Malaspina, Palagonia, and Libertà, areas buffered from the dilapidated old city to the south and east by a commercial area and several monumental public buildings, and fanning out from the tree-lined Via della Libertà. The characteristic architecture of the New Palermo – a mixture of sleek high-rises and turn of the century "Liberty"-style villas – contrasts with the crumbling old city and the drab housing developments on the periphery.

The mothers as well as the fathers of the students are steadily and profitably employed professionals and high-ranking bureaucrats. The students themselves are bound for university studies and similar careers. While working people in Albergheria and Zisa live alongside African immigrants, the bourgeoisie tend to encounter mainly Asian immigrants. For them, Filipinos, Cape Verdians, Mauritians, and Sri Lankans represent not neighbors, co-workers, or competitors, but trustworthy household staff. These students occasionally meet foreigners through cultural associations or at events such as the annual Festa dell'Unità, an important cultural fair held in late summer in cities throughout Italy and sponsored by the Italian Communist Party (PCI – Partito Comunista Italiano).[1] However, they primarily meet immigrants as domestic workers in their homes and in the homes of their friends.

By contrast, the University of Palermo students surveyed tend to come from working and petty bourgeois backgrounds in the small agricultural towns of the interior, from which so many Sicilians emigrated over the past century. While the parents of the typical Ruggero II student may be high-level bureaucrats or teachers, a university student's mother is typically a housewife and his or her father could well be an agricultural day laborer or a local merchant. These students are good examples of the recent general trend in class formation in rural Sicily from working-class to petty bourgeois status. They are obtaining a higher education but still speak the Sicilian dialect as well as Italian. They have familiarity if not firsthand experience of emigration, but probably would not follow their uncles' and fathers' trajectories to northern factories. Their friends, too, tend be educated, white-collar employees, doctors, and teachers. Assisted by a university librarian who was well known among students, I gave the questionnaire to students at a student dormitory and university center catering to students from out of town, located near the Albergheria parish church. The group consisted of 15 males and 11 females between 19 and 30 years of age.

As we will see, both student groups presented a sophisticated, universalist, and consistently pro-immigrant stance at odds with the ambivalence and inconsistency of working-class views. Because these views were expressed in a social context, representation of self and Other is dialectical. The bourgeois Palermitan describes himself or herself as the tolerant, enlightened citizen in constrast to the exploited and ignorant denizen of the popular quarter; at the same time, the bourgeois interprets immigrants in relation to the desirability of intercultural exchange and the "beauty" of a multiracial Italy. Working people, for their part, contrast the cheap and self-aggrandizing talk of "fine" people with the competition and hardship immigration brings to their own unrecognized struggles; and they contrast their skills and contributions to Italy to the unskilled foreign workers who make unjust but, they fear, convincing demands on the Italian state. Differences in terminology signal this divide. One of my neighbors in Albergheria depicted this difference with characteristically popular flair and with a vocabulary which recalls working people's self-presentation as virtuous bearers of traditional culture:

In popular areas we call them *tuichi* [Turks] whereas in via [della] Libertà and [via] Strasbourgo they use finer names like *extracomunitari* and *immigrati di colore*. They think of us as impolite and as criminals, and there are some of those here. They think they're finer and more polished, but they have "the horns" [are cuckolds]. The wife gives them to the husband and they like it!

I asked him if this had anything to do with immigration and he replied no, he was just describing the bourgeoisie.

Of race and racism

The views of what my neighbor called the "fine" people and their children – as well as those of the university students – typically reflect those of most Italian intellectuals and institutions concerned with immigration. With regard to race and racism, they draw on the post-Holocaust consensus that the very concept of race is questionable, and that racist theory and practice are immoral. Because the campaign against racism has set the tone for much debate over immigration during the past several years, a willingness to worry about the possibilities of racism in Italy serves to define membership in the circle of the lettered.

Review of the six pertinent survey questions shows the familiar promotion of racial equality along with the condemnation of *razzismo* among the student samples. (See the Appendix for the questionnaire.) These questions, which I employed in the last chapter as a diagnostic of working-class attitudes on race and racism, concern the following themes: (1) the importance of race; (2) the validity of race as a criterion for restricting immigration; (3) Sicilian–immigrant intermarriage; (4) Sicilian, as compared with immigrant, migration history; (5) comparison between different immigrant populations; and (6) the responsibility of immigrants for the problems of Palermo.[2]

1 Race, for these students, has no bearing on the merits of individuals or groups. While almost 10 percent of the students at the Zisa school agreed with the statement "A person's race is important and the white race is best," at Ruggero II and the University of Palermo all (save one college prankster) chose the reply: "A person's race is not important." One high-school student even corrected the very phrasing of the question by disputing the validity of the concept of race: "Le persone non hanno razze" ("People do not belong to races").

2 Similarly, none of the high-school students would restrict immigration to protect the white race, while the one university student who so objected probably did so by mistake, because this response contradicted all his other answers.

3 Again, all students agreed that intermarriage between Sicilians and foreigners was happening, or would happen. One Ruggero II student, however, stated her intention never so to marry, and one

university man pointed to the difficulties of marriage across cultures. While working-class samples also thought intermarriage probable, these students typically went on to endorse it. One high-school student described it as a means for achieving the goal of racial equality:

> I think it would be beautiful. I hope that it happens as soon as possible because I believe in a multiracial and multi-ethnic society in which all are equal.[3]

4   When asked to evaluate immigrants against Sicilians, most high-school students (34 out of 43) and almost all the university students (22 out of 24) saw the two populations as "the same." While 6 out of 43 high-school students and one university student judged to be immigrants "more honest and industrious" than Sicilians, only 3 out of 43 at the high school and 1 out of 24 at the university described them as "dirty and dangerous." (One of the high-school students' negative appraisals was at odds with the rest of her questionnaire.)[4]

5   Reactions to the question concerning the relative merits and demerits of different immigrant groups show an unwillingness to stereotype. At the university, the majority (15 out of 25) judged immigrants to be just like them, 7 out of 25 did not know, and 3 acknowledged differences without describing them. At Ruggero II, most students (21 out of 44) did not respond or did not know; a large minority (18 out of 44) dismissed the idea of comparison by saying that we are all the same or by saying that the qualities of immigrants hinge on the possibilities Italians offer them. Finally, 5 out of 44 saw differences. Of those who offered examples, 2 described Asians as honest, while 3 described North Africans as bad (*imbroglioni pericolosi*, "dangerous cheats," one called North African vendors), and one sees Africans as "good people."

6   The final question asked respondents to rank the following phenomena from most to least responsible for Palermo's chronic unemployment and lack of industry: mafia, national government, regional and city government, the global economy, African and Asian immigration, and Palermitans themselves. Responses here coincided with those of earlier samples. As in the Zisa sample, high-school students pointed to the suffocating triangle of mafia, national government, and regional and city governments – with 13, 12, and 11 first-place votes, respectively. University students recalled the Albergheria sample by isolating the dual menace of

mafia and national government (12.5 and 11.5 first-place votes, respectively). All university students gave immigrants the lowest ranking (fifth or sixth place) of blame. At Ruggero II the overwhelming majority (41 out of 44) assigned immigrants the least responsibility, and only 1 out of 44 gave them a fourth place, and 2 out of 44 gave them third places.

These high-school and university students, then, consistently express an explicit anti-racism. As much as differences in vocabulary, these politically charged understandings and goals separate them from the Zisa and Albergheria samples. The majority of those in the working-class sample reject racial and racist categorizations of those whom they call "Turks." In contrast, highly educated students not only reject these categories, they decry intolerance and racism, and envision a future multiracial Italy in which "immigrants of color" enjoy parity with Italians. Ideas about the hardships endured by foreigners illustrate this distinctive preoccupation with racism and intolerance. All of the university students, for example, describe immigrants as suffering intolerance, marginality, ghettoization, and racism. As one woman put it, foreign workers are "a world apart and barely tolerated." High-school students were more critical yet. The majority (34 out of 43) describe immigrants suffering intolerance and exploitation, and almost a third (9 out of 34) of those specify racism. (As among the working-class, sex in the high-school and university groups does not correlate with significant differences in attitudes.) The working-class respondents, for their part, also note maltreatment of immigrants, but focus more on economic exploitation. It is not enough to say, as I did earlier, that race is without significance for high-school and university students. On the contrary, race – and the accompanying complex of related topics such as anti-racism, tolerance, and multiracialism – now plays an important and defining role in the political ideology of the majority of educated Italians who are to the left of the neo-Fascist Italian Social Movement (MSI – Movimento Sociale Italiano).[5]

Views of immigrants on the labor market
This fairly consistent political ideology, broad as it is, also colors interpretations of immigrant participation on the labor market. Whereas working Palermitans typically make contradictory assessments of this participation, high-school and university students see immigrants as simply workers located at the exploited bottom of the occupational hierarchy. Their appraisals of immigrants and "black" work, intolerance, hiring, and

the consequences for the labor market remain uncomplicated by ambivalence.

Ruggero II and university students see both immigrants and local poor suffering from the exploitation of "black" work, although a few qualify this by saying that locals' wages drop under the competitive pressure of foreign workers. Benefitting from this state of affairs are employers, according to Ruggero II and university respondents. For the university respondents, mafia and government also benefit. As I noted earlier, most of the people in these samples see immigrants as enduring exploitation and intolerance, with high school students in particular identifying the problem of Sicilian *razzismo*.

These students, like those in the working-class samples, overwhelmingly agree on hiring foreign workers in response to the following question: "If you were an employer, for what reason would you hire or not hire an immigrant?" Some 37 out of 43 high-school and 22 out of 25 university students would hire an immigrant, as would 42 out of 50 people in the Zisa sample, and 12 out of 14 in the Albergheria sample. These results differ from the working-class ones in that many fewer – 2 out of 43 and 1 out of 25 at the high school and university, respectively, versus 8 out of 50 in Zisa and 2 out of 14 in Albergheria, respectively – object to hiring foreigners. Reasons for hiring immigrants differed between the two schools, as well. Of the 37 who would so hire at Ruggero II, 25 would do it because of the qualities of the individual, 11 because they are better workers, and only 1 because they are cheaper. Of the 22 university students so disposed, 16 would do so because of the individual qualities of foreigners and 6 because they work for less.[6]

Finally, the questionnaire presented two alternative interpretations of the effect of foreign workers on the labor market. While the working-class informants in Zisa and Albergheria split over this question – notwithstanding their willingness to enjoy the benefits of hiring immigrants – the high-school and university ones do not. A majority of 28 out of 38 and 19 out of 24 at Ruggero II and the university, respectively, endorse the view that immigrants have little effect on the labor market because they do jobs refused by local people.

In sum, students consistently interpret foreign workers as a novel lower stratum of the working class. For them, immigrants do the "most humble" jobs refused or abandoned by Palermitans, cause little disturbance to the labor market, and, like the Sicilian poor, find exploitation and little security in the undocumented work so prevalent in this city of abuses. True to their ideological predilection, they tend to see "immigrants of color" and "blacks" as suffering as much from racism as from economic exploitation. Working Palermitans, by contrast, see the undocumented work of "Turks" as exploitation, which is detrimental to them as well as to the foreigners themselves.

Consistency of interpretation also sets these students apart from working-class ambivalence. Working Palermitans simultaneously recognize and deny the dual labor market. Because the highly educated students, particularly the elite group at Ruggero II, are implicated not as potential co-workers or competitors but as potential employers of immigrants, they can regard the phenomenon from another perspective. It would be unthinkable for these young men and women to express the conflict of working people, who, as we saw in the previous chapter, struggle when confronted with the contradictions in their accounts of the dual labor market and of Sicilian emigration as compared with current immigration.

On the contrary, more characteristic of well-educated Palermitans is the calm detachment of an architect I chanced to encounter at the vacation house of a mutual friend. After a refreshing swim in the turquoise waters off a rocky, protected shore, we climbed up steps cut into the hillside to the cool terrace. There, over pasta and champagne, he asked me about my research, about the effect of "immigrants of color" on the lives and jobs of the *popolino*, or "little people." I told him that in my opinion the effect was negligible because immigrants had filled the interstitial and undermanned sectors of the labor market. He agreed with this assessment and went on to discuss the changing racial composition of Europe (for this immigration affected all of western Europe and not just Italy). The innate tolerance of Sicilians towards foreigners, and the question of racism, also came up:

I can tell you that I am not racist, that it offends my principles, but I cannot say exactly how I would act if my children decided to marry an immigrant. Perhaps you have seen the movie, *Guess Who's Coming to Dinner?*, in which a girl brings home her black boyfriend, to the consternation of her parents. Great movie! More champagne?

Of emigrants and immigrants
Students approach the issues of Sicilian emigration and Third-World immigration with the same equanimity and positive attitudes that they bring to all other aspects of the immigration question. While people from Albergheria and Zisa characteristically comprehend the plight of immigrants but maintain that their inferiority makes them incomparable to Sicilian emigrants, students do not hestitate to equate the experience of

the two populations and to draw conclusions about the need for greater immigrant rights and recognition.

Questionnaire results show that high-school and university students view Sicilian emigration in much the same way as do those in the working-class samples. They too describe emigration as compelled by the miserable living and working conditions, the terrible *fame,* or "hunger," that haunted so many peasants and urban poor in Sicily and the Italian south up to the very recent past; and they identify as "miserable" and "most humble" the low-paying jobs in mines, factories, construction, and services performed by Sicilians in the north and abroad.

In their responses to the two questions concerning emigrant experience in the United States and in northern Italy, the university students exhibit their familiarity with the topic. For instance, 14 out of 26 enumerate such problems for Sicilians in the United States as presumed association with the mafia, stigmatization for their origin, competition with other poor groups, and strife with African Americans. Fewer (5 out of 26) describe life there as without difficulty; about the same number (7 out of 26) do not know. Most high-school students (29 out of 43), by contrast, either fail to respond or admit they do not know. Only 1 out of 43 describes life there as trouble free, and 14 out of 43 list such problems as language, reputed association with the mafia, even racism.

Both groups of (petty) bourgeois students, like many working Palermitans, portray the situation of emigrants in the north of Italy as one of exploitation and marginality. However, many of the high-school students (27 out of 44), who usually answered questions in dutiful detail, noted this but give few examples, while a large majority of the university students (20 out of 26) drew on their familiarity with emigration to produce a rich account. Indeed, theirs is a veritable litany of the indignities suffered by fellow Sicilians in the industrial triangle: marginality, humiliation, living in barracks, maltreatment as inferior, and – noteworthy with regard to interpretations of current immigration – racism. They also describe low wages and "black" work, dirty and dangerous jobs refused by locals, and accusations of "stealing" work from local workers.[7]

Interviews in Albergheria revealed a profound resentment of the anti-southernism pervasive in the north. While I did not interview those in these high-school and university samples on this problem, numerous friendships and acquaintances with professionals in Palermo and rural western Sicily permit me to make some generalizations.

These Sicilians, like working Palermitans, resent the all-too-common caricatures of southerners as mafiosi, welfare-state dependents, and backward. They chafe at the solemn biannual announcement of the Italian Statistical Institute (ISTAT – Istituto Nazionale di Statistica) that the southern birth rate exceeds the northern one. In addition to comments about the corruption of Rome – "the fish starts to stink at the head" – they point to the century-old alliance of national government and northern capital which has worked to draw resources from the south to industrialize the north. For northerners to disparage as lazy and somehow inferior the southerners who furnished so much labor power to the factories of the industrial triangle seems, to them, to border on *razzismo*. Especially distressing is the Lombard League,[8] with its alarmist rhetoric about the national state being taken over by southerners, the too-fecund south, and its proposal to separate the south from the north by means of three large federal states in the place of the current regions. Such steps would constitute the political enactment of a mean-spirited anti-southernism. A well-educated Sicilian who spent many years organizing alternative communes in Tuscany once told me of the pervasive disparagement of *terroni* there. Tuscans constantly surprised and offended him with their compliments to the effect that he was certainly a remarkable exception to the rule of the lazy and ignorant Sicilian.

Yet these Sicilian professionals also measure their resentment of the *terrone* stereotype with a realistic, and therefore sad and cynical, appraisal of the Sicilian political and, as it were, "immoral" economy. While working Palermitans tend to deflect ultimate responsibility for the Sicilian mafia to Rome, these people note the undeniable power of the mafia in Sicily, where corrupt politicians, common bribery, and disrespect for the institution of the state are rampant. In effect, they admit that the League is right to denounce the southern politicians who have long diverted state monies earmarked for the development of the south to friends and clients. I recall a conversation I had with a priest serving the local and foreign poor in the *centro storico*. He described Sicilians as "parasites" on the industrial north who aim only to "occupy and not produce jobs." Finally, I asked if he was Sicilian himself. He answered "yes" and went on to say how immigrants, like the Sicilian emigrants before them, represent the most productive people of their respective countries, people who leave suffocating political and economic regimes to find better opportunities elsewhere. For him, the northern stereotype of the lazy and dependent south is sadly accurate, for this described what was left behind.

In particular, many Sicilian professionals and intellectuals deplore the general *degrado*, or "degradation," that debilitates Sicily. *Degrado*, a concept which gained salience during the profusion of critical reform movements of the "Palermo Spring," refers to the sorry ensemble of physical dilapidation, infrastructural disorder, administrative neglect and corruption, as well as acquiescence to mafia rule and widespread attachment to the giant clientelistic food chain linked to government spending. Former mayor Leoluca Orlando encapsulated this critique and the idea of reform with his suggestion of replacing the "culture of belonging" to party and patrons with the "culture of being" responsible, participating citizens (Settineri and Governali 1990: 76).

For these Sicilians, the north represents not just an oppressor but also bureaucratic efficiency, participatory democracy, and meritocracy. With pain, they see these standards, which they have come to call their own, subverted and mocked on a daily basis in their homeland as jobs and scholarships are awarded on the basis of patronage and not merit. The majority, of course, probably pay lip service to these criticisms and go about their business with vigor, but many whom I met react with bitterness, resignation, and cynicism. Some carry on out of necessity; others withdraw from their chosen fields into the security of a minor bureacratic position untouched by compromise.

The high-school and university respondents describe many aspects of current immigration in much the same way as respondents of the working class. According to them, entering Africans and Asians are escaping poverty and oppression, undertake the jobs abandoned by Palermitans, and endure indifference, intolerance, and even racism. However, in the highly educated samples, people typically and predictably place individual migration in such broader contexts as global demographic trends, underdevelopment and political repression in the Third World, and the attraction of political freedom and consumerism in the West. At times, for me, their answers recall classroom discussions in graduate school, as with this university woman who sketches the causes of immigration in broad materialist terms:

I do not know a lot about it. But I imagine that they [countries sending migrants] suffer the ravages of the Western economy which expands across the planet, destroying old equilibria, concentrating wealth in small areas, and plundering natural and human resources wherever it can.[9]

Analyzing immigration in relation to global processes of wealth and power, students make an explicit comparison or equation of emigration with immigration. In this, they mirror the opinions of institutional spokespersons and public officials concerned with immigration with whom they share many similarities in class experience and education.

While working Palermitans grapple with the unresolvable contradictions between their own emigration history and that of Africans and Asians, these students do not hesitate to accept the comparison and to pursue conclusions regarding immigrant rights. It is reflective of this tendency to equate the two migrations that almost a quarter (6 out of 26) of those in the university sample answered the survey question on the causes on immigration by stating that immigrants come "for the same reasons" that Sicilians left.

In a certain sense, then, high-school and university students view immigration through the moral lens of the Sicilian emigrant experience, the "historical memory" that institutional representatives often regard as key for any program of tolerance and acceptance of immigrants. The broader ideological stance of supporting immigration gives salience to this "memory." I will suggest later that this ideology stems from Italy's strong dual traditions of concern for the oppressed – Catholic universalism and the internationalism of the left.

Responses to four survey questions eliciting comparisons of the two migrations illustrate the consistently pro-immigrant position of the bourgeois student samples.

1   The first question asks whether immigrants will contribute to Italian development through their labor and culture, or will instead take resources away from Italians. High-school (33.5 out of 43) and especially university (23 out of 26) students saw immigrants as contributors (2 out of 26 university students said it depends on future political developments).[10]

2   The second question presents three choices: (1) to support regulated immigration because 27 million Italians emigrated abroad for work in this century, or not to support it because of (2) potential contamination of the white race, or (3) joblessness among Italians. Again, the slim majorities of Zisa (31 out of 55) and Albergheria (7.5 out of 14) selecting the first choice pale when compared with the overwhelming support in the high-school (34 out of 42) and university (23 out of 25) samples. Of the latter samples, university students once again stand out for championing the cause of immigration: while 8 out of 43 high-school students objected to immigration on the grounds of Italian unemployment, only 1 out of 25 university students so objected. (This student, who objected on racial grounds, possibly erred because he did so in contradiction to all his other answers.)

3   The third question asks whether the national government acted responsibly with regard to its own citizens when it passed Law #39 in 1990 (the so-called "Martelli law"), which legalized many of the foreign workers already present in Italy. Ruggero II students showed a surprising ignorance of the law, with fully three-quarters (33 out of 44) leaving the question blank or saying they did not know.[11] Notwithstanding their lack of knowledge of the law, high-school and university students again expressed full support for immigrant rights. All 11 of the high-school students expressing an opinion did so in support of the law. While 18 out of 26 university students supported it, and 6 out of 26 admitted ignorance, only 2 out of 26 viewed it as irresponsible.[12]

The popular outrage over the "strike of the immigrants" described in the previous chapter could not be more at odds with the culture of political protest so important to Italian university life. This radical tradition dates from the early 1960s, when educational-reform legislation more than doubled the student population in Italian universities. Thwarted by inadequate facilities and elitism, skeptical of the postwar Italian economic "miracle," and inspired by communism in China and elsewhere, Italian university students revolted in 1967–8, giving impetus to subsequent struggles in factories (Ginsborg 1990: 298–309). Although tempered over time, this radical heritage continues to inform political opinion among university students.

4   The fourth and final question asks whether, and how, the historical emigration of Sicilians abroad is comparable with current immigration to Sicily. While the working-class samples, exhibiting their profound and signature ambivalence towards immigrants, saw more difference than similarity in the two migrations, these students saw more similarity. At Ruggero II, 31 out of 44 supported the idea of similarity, which puts the present immigration in a very positive light (versus the 7 out of 44 who did not, and the 6 out of 44 who admitted ignorance). Among university students, 20 out of 26 supported the idea, while just 2 out of 26 repudiated it (and 4 out of 26 pleaded ignorance). These two groups tended to describe similarity in terms of a push–pull model: of poverty inducing people to seek a better life available somewhere else. At the same time, they noted such differences as the superior education of current immigrants, and the magnitude and novelty of Third-World debt – characteristics that place current immigrants in an

even more acceptable position. Indeed, the few who argued for the dissimilarity of the two migrations did so not to stamp the new immigrants as inferior and ultimately incomparable, as working Palermitans might. Rather they pointed out that immigrants, not emigrants, suffer racism, or that the new immigration has created a novel multiracial situation. One young high-school student, for example, argued the case for dissimilarity this way:

> The political, economic, social, and cultural contexts are too different to lump the two movements into a single case. . . . The two movements, however, can be considered similar at the level of human misery, hope, and experience.[13]

Even dissent on this question reflects a political orientation favorable to immigrant rights. It is to the explanation of this characteristic support of foreigners' rights and place in Sicilian society that I now turn.

The four paradigms of immigration

The professional bourgeoisie of Palermo, to which many of these high-school and university students do or will belong, draw on one or more of what I shall call "paradigmatic" understandings of immigration. I treat four broad tendencies as paradigms, namely: religious solidarity, labor solidarity, labor-market rationality, and anti-immigration or the "new racism." Characteristic understandings, goals, and initiatives define each paradigm, and each is associated with particular intellectual voices and political camps. While I will discuss these in more detail later, I introduce them here so that I can suggest how and why they resonate with people in the (petty) bourgeois samples.

The paradigm of religious solidarity draws on traditions of universalism in the Catholic Church, traditions honed by recent progressive activity in the Third World and in pioneering work with immigrants in Italy. According to this interpretation, immigrants flee poverty and repression at home, take up work refused by Italians, and suffer neglect, even racism. Without a doubt the most important work of the various organs of the church, particularly the Caritàs, has been to offer homeless and/or jobless foreigners the food and shelter which local governments usually fail to provide. Proponents of this paradigm exhort Italians to overcome their fear of the Other which underwrites racism and to embrace immigrants as brothers under God, whatever their religion. Immigration thus presents itself as a challenge and opportunity for a multiracial society characterized by mutual religious tolerance and intellectual enrichment. Representatives of churches and intellectuals also routinely press the government to act on matters of legislation and aid. In Palermo, Caritàs, the Italian Christian Workers' Association (ACLI – Associazioni Cristiane Lavoratori Italiani), the Presbyterian Church (Chiesa Valdese), and especially the Salesian Order, prominently articulate this paradigm through their work.

The paradigm of labor solidarity unites various traditions of the Italian left, linking labor organizations at home and the theme of international solidarity abroad to critiques of Third-World underdevelopment and capitalism. Left-wing political parties and their cultural organizations, trade-union leaders, and associated intellectuals champion this interpretation, which is widely expressed in Italy and Palermo. According to this understanding, a volatile combination of demographic trends, political repression, and national debt drive people from the poor "South" of the world to its rich "North" where they find work at the bottom of the labor market. A cynical acceptance of the exploitation of immigrants, in addition to a general fear of the racial Other, causes intolerance and racism in Italy. Proponents of this paradigm, like those of the preceding one, vaunt a multiracial Italy, although they stress immigrants' economic contribution and herald the goal of secular fraternity. They propose to achieve this goal by passing legislation for immigrant rights, enrolling foreigners in trade unions, and publicizing the cause of anti-racism. In Palermo, the unions, particularly the CGIL (Confederazione Generale Italiana del Lavoro),[14] and cultural associations such as the ARCI (Associazione Ricreativa Culturale Italiana)[15] articulate this paradigm. On the other hand, political parties, including, ironically, the Communist Party, remain silent. Possibly its small size, position of weakness outside of local and regional government, and affiliation in the 1970s with construction concerns involved in mafia corruption (Schneider and Schneider 1997) explain the silence of the PCI (Italian Communist Party) on immigration, as on other matters.

The third paradigm, that of labor-market rationality, finds its influential champions in government and business. According to this view, factors such as Third-World debt and population growth work to direct an unremitting stream of potential immigrants towards the rich West. These people represent both a threat, to be controlled by restrictive immigration legislation at home and development programs abroad, and a reserve of cheap and temporary labor, to be utilized as needed. The law on immigration, which both temporarily closes the border and facilitates the integration of foreign workers already present into the labor force, serves the dual interests of this paradigm's proponents. In the region of Sicily there is as yet no legislation on immigration, as required by Law #39. Nevertheless, there is a widespread understanding among Sicilian police and politicians that North Africans on tourist visas are essential to the region's agricultural production. Proponents of the law denounce intolerance as the child of ignorance, bound to lessen in time as the immigrants become assimilated. However, by ceding jobs and services to immigrants, they also run the political risk of enraging jobless Italians and inviting attacks by anti-immigrant entrepreneurs such as the Lombard League (LL) and the neo-fascist Italian Social Movement (MSI).

At some level, all three of these paradigms validate immigrant rights on the basis of the experience of Italian emigration. Catholics would receive foreigners not just out of reciprocal duty but out of Christian love. Unionists would strengthen the working-class movement by unionizing foreign workers. Government and business interests would grant a limited number of immigrants the opportunity to live and work in Italy for reasons of labor-market efficiency. These arguments, voiced at the national level, find a particular resonance among educated Sicilians.

The fourth paradigm, unlike the others, is resolutely anti-immigrant. The successful and clamorous Lombard League proposes to address immigration by rescinding the rights guaranteed by the 1990 law and by promoting repatriation. Proponents of this paradigm recognize the crushing circumstances driving immigration, circumstances which constitute a veritable moral call to receive immigrants for many Catholics and leftists. But like "new racists" throughout western Europe, the League bridles at foreigners taking work away from nationals, rejects the notion of duty towards immigrants, and recoils in horror at the thought of racial and ethnic intermingling. This paradigm, like the first two, harks back to questions of race and racism. For these *leghisti* who loudly claim to be "not racist," immigration (and therefore all who condone it) actually causes intolerance and racism by provoking in Italians the natural human urge to protect their ethnicity and territory. In a move worthy of Le Pen, League spokespeople cynically suggest that even immigrants would be better served by repatriation, because it would return them to their natural unit, their own ethnic group or nation. Needless to say, neither the Lombard League nor the other less influential leagues, all of which demonize southerners more than foreigners, claim many adherents in Palermo (see chapter 1, note 9).

Explaining adherence to paradigms
Of the preceding paradigms, the first three were dominant in Italy in early 1990, although the fourth was gaining substantial ground in the north, as I

discuss in the next chapter. The views of high-school and university students in Palermo are particularly informed by the paradigm of labor solidarity, while the bourgeoisie as a whole probably takes as much from ideas about labor market rationality. While I met few Palermitans who ground opinions about race and immigration in religious thought, proponents of this paradigm contribute beyond their numbers to the debate in Palermo. Whatever their paradigm of choice, not a few Palermitans invoke the duty of former emigrants to receive current immigrants.

Class and education do, however, influence the enthusiasm for paradigms favorable to immigration and diversity. In Sicily, as in Europe and the United States, people with better jobs and more education typically express more tolerance on race than those with lower-paying jobs and less education (Amodio 1989; Bonifazi and Golini 1989; Guala 1989; Italia-razzismo 1990; Van Dijk 1987). They are aware of the norms against racism and are skilled at presentation of self and Other in socially acceptable ways. Furthermore, by expressing tolerance, they present themselves as progressive citizens whose enlightenment contrasts favorably with the ignorance and tendency towards intolerance of working people (Van Dijk 1987).

The enthusiasm of the high-school and university students for the paradigms of tolerance also reflects Italian political culture. Early debate on race and immigration in Italy was distinguished by the dominance of pro-immigrant positions. Moreover, adherence to pro-immigrant paradigms, particularly to that of labor solidarity, has become an important and defining feature of membership of self-defined progressive circles. In the classical high-school and university milieux of 1990, such views were *de rigueur*, as the survey data show. Further, because self-representation is dialectical, such views not only serve to present themselves but also serve to distinguish their adherents from others. Thus students contrast their radical racial politics to the ill-informed and potential intolerance of the working classes, on one hand, and to the opportunism of the local elite who benefit from the class structure and racial antagonism, on the other. (The bourgeoisie as a whole also holds interpretations favorable to immigration, but in a less adamant form.) These high-school and university students come to learn and articulate such interpretations in school, through the media (especially the print media), and through participation in the activities of a multitude of political and cultural associations sponsored by the Church, the Left, and organized labor.

In addition to the influences of Italian political culture, certain aspects of Sicilian history and culture also give salience to these broad paradigms.

Palermitan professionals, particularly members of the cultural elite that exercise most influence on the high-school and university students, often base calls for tolerance on the island's multicultural past and on Sicilian emigrant experience. These historical legacies are seen as explaining current tolerance or as moral precedents worthy of emulation. The symbolic efficacy of such local models explains part of their attraction; their capacity to convey complicated themes in a concise and resonant manner makes them attractive to those who would organize and publicize the cause. Perhaps more importantly, they highlight memorable achievements in Sicilian history and mark Sicilians off from other Italians, whether as descendants of a plurality of cultures and races who crossed the Mediterranean, or as those whose understanding of migration stems from the pain and excitement of the experience itself. Here, too, are claims to the moral superiority of those who suffer unjustly, which I found central to working-class self-representation. According to Alessandro Portelli (1989), southern Italians identify their repression and anger with that of black Americans. He quotes the famous (white) Italian sprinter, Pietro Mennea, who proclaimed, "Io vinco le Olimpiadi perché sono meridionale" ("I win the Olympics because I am a southerner"). For Portelli this means, "ho la stessa rabbia storica dei neri americani" ("I have the same historical rage as black Americans") (Portelli 1989: 96–7). Even among those Palermitans most cynical about the ever-present corruption it is possible to hear talk of a distinctive Sicilian tolerance which contrasts favorably to northern intolerance and self-satisfaction.

Of contradiction and consistency

In sum, questionnaire and other data show that high-school and university students regard immigrants in a favorable light. They decry racism and support anti-racism; they see immigrants as contributors and not as threats; they favor immigrant rights, and anticipate a multiracial Italy in which "all are equal." In general, members of the Palermo bourgeoisie also adhere to similar, albeit much diluted, views. Such views, I have suggested, derive from and contribute to nation-wide paradigms, but are also given immediacy by aspects of Sicilian culture and history. Finally, coherence characterizes these interpretations. The status of the paradigms as important themes in political debate, their constant reworking in the face of criticism and new information, and the education and political mobilization of their adherents – all contribute to their characteristic consistency and sophistication. This systematic point of view, grounded in explicit and political ideologies, approximates to Frank Reeves' (1983) concept of "specialized political discourse," in contrast to the "weakly structured" and possibly inconsistent "general discourse" of working Palermitans.

Yet these views, contrastive in their consistency and sophistication to those of working people, are not free from contradiction. This is especially true if I broaden the analysis to include the bourgeoisie as a whole (and occasionally Italians as a whole), and introduce data other than question-naire results. My impressions of the Palermo bourgeoisie in general come from a snowball sample of mostly professional people whom I met through friends and acquaintances. The contradictions which emerge are not so much contradictions internal to paradigms of immigration as contradictory and inconsistent ideas and practices. In particular, ideas and practices regarding politics, popular culture, and labor relations illustrate such discrepancies.

The Italia-razzismo (1990) study of Italian understandings of immi-grants, for example, reveals telling inconsistencies between ideology and understandings. Despite their self-professed egalitarian and "anti-racist" ideologies, many in this survey know little and have no curiosity about immigrants. They attribute a battery of unfavorable qualities to immi-grants, including an unrestrained sexual appetite, immaturity, and lack of discipline (Italia-razzismo 1990: 7–9). The study also reveals Italians to lack clear models for interacting with foreigners.

This discrepancy between rhetoric and action is not confined to the average Italian, however: it also characterizes the realm of politics, where inaction gives the lie to the rhetoric of equality. The attraction of the common Italian self-representation as inherently tolerant – *italiani, brava gente* ("Italians, a good people") – stems from Italy's strong tradition of internationalism. People remember the partisan movement whose contri-bution to ending Fascism erases or mitigates another memory: Mussolini's invasion and colonization of East and North Africa, the surrendering of Jews to the Nazis, and the adoption of Hitlerian racial laws. The postwar tendency to condemn racial inequality throughout the world from the safety of a fairly homogeneous society also influences contemporary anti-racism in Italy (Balbo 1990; Bocca 1988; Portelli 1989).

There is no reason to think that debate in Sicily has surmounted these (and other) obstacles to clear statements of theory and action. Argument by declaration and a romantic outlook characterize the slogans of the institutional representatives and the well educated in Palermo. Some recall the periods of Arab and Norman rule of 800–1,000 years ago as a model and precursor of today's multiracial and multicultural Sicily. They point to

Arab technology and architecture, and to the Normans' even-handed rule over distinct ethnic populations as exemplary. Intellectuals with little emigration experience also exhort working-class Sicilians to accept immigrants with a good deal more good will than northern Italians have accepted them.

Italian popular cultural images of the Other also clash with the rhetoric of multiracial equality. For example, Arabs are portrayed as untrustworthy and possessed by fanatical Islam, while blacks are seen as both glamorous and savage (Gallini 1989; Leschiutta 1989; Portelli 1989). Because racial stereotypes so often focus on the body, at once the most natural and cultural of objects, ideas about sexuality often accompany them. Pictures of beautiful dark-skinned women grace advertisements for coffee, underscoring the sensual pleasures of the foreign product. Immigrant women with whom I spoke in Palermo complained about the Italian stereotype of the sexy and lusty black woman; theirs are stories of relentless leers and propositions. A priest, speaking to a group of Cape Verdian women, expresses this prejudice most clearly:

You must always be on your guard. When will the devil attack you? He knows that you are weak. Perhaps you will think that he will attack with regard to sex. But the devil knows you are weak in this regard, that there is little need for him to help you, that you can sin all by yourselves.[16]   (*quoted in Crisantino 1992: 151*)

While it is difficult to assess the extent of essentialist discourse in Italy, I argue that it does indeed condition interpretations of immigrants among most people. Italians of all classes are influenced by stereotypes. They may understand them to be untrue characterizations, but necessary dramatic characters for fiction; they may treat them with irony, as intellectuals do; or they may create and disseminate them, without an overt racist thought entering their heads. Ultimately, however, these pratices tend to perpetuate a hegemonic definition of the non-white Other as fundamentally different and inferior. Discussion of popular racist stereotypes has a particular bearing on the question of bourgeois attitudes to race and immigration because, in contrast to the working class, this class proclaims itself to be anti-racist.

Labor relations between Italians and the immigrants who are their servants illustrate how power and ideology interact on a daily level. It is here that the class position of the bourgeoisie and popular stereotypes of the Other show their contradictions most clearly. The dual participation of the bourgeois on the labor market, as both highly remunerated employee and employer, establishes a form of contradictory dominance over the foreign worker, in this case over the Asian and Cape Verdian women who predominate in the domestic labor market. The arrival of these women coincided with the withdrawal of local women from this market. So great was the resulting demand in this sector that some bourgeois families actually sent airline tickets to prospective *colf* in, for example, Mauritius (Crisantino 1992: 33, 35, 133). Now, almost twenty years later, the presence of foreigners in Palermo has eased this "crisis" considerably. A visit to a domestic employment agency such as API–COLF will, after a relatively short delay, procure the services of a *colf*.

For Palermo's bourgeoisie, then, immigrants represent not co-workers, competitors, and neighbors, but a convenient pool of domestic servants. While working people see immigrants as threats to their already tenuous security, the affluent greet them as reliable and useful workers whose presence in the home carries a certain distinction. According to a woman from Madagascar, the convenient relationship explains the atmosphere of tolerance in rich New Palermo. For a small sum, foreign women have made life more comfortable for countless bourgeois Palermitan women and afforded them prestige; furthermore, these workers do not draw attention to themselves, or agitate for greater rights (Crisantino 1992: 21). Filipinos, whose high status and pay relative to other foreign *colf* are based in part on their organization, constitute a partial exception to the rule.

Nevertheless, this bourgeois tolerance, born of convenience as well as of political orientation, is not free from contradiction, namely that of saying and doing, between which, Italians say, "there lies half the sea" ("Tra dire e fare c'è mezzo mare"). As Teun Van Dijk (1987) and Philomena Essed (1991) have shown, bourgeois behavior often does not measure up to bourgeois expressions of tolerance. My conversations with immigrant women and *colf* agency officials suggest that in the early days of immigration not a few Palermitans exploited vulnerable foreign live-in domestics through underpayment, long hours, and a refusal to legalize their residency and work status. Some of the women whose stories were collected by Amelia Crisantino reported that their employers rarely let them out of the house and treated them as servants only, not as people (e.g., Crisantino 1992: 136–7). A Mauritian woman describes the jealousy and possessiveness of such a *padrona*: "The [Sicilian] women wanted them [the good foreign domestics] forever, never wanted them to marry, so they would not have to adjust to another woman"[17] (Crisantino 1992: 50). But the immigrants with whom I spoke, like those interviewed by Crisantino, rarely complained of "racism," or overt discrimination and hostility. Rather, they objected to Sicilian smugness, labor-market position, and legal impediments, which together confined them to domestic labor, leaving their skills untapped, and limiting their opportunities and contributions.

Gradually, exploitation of foreign domestics became more difficult and less common. Immigrants came to understand their situation as they increasingly rented apartments with others, outside of their places of work, and met Sicilians concerned with their plight. Legislation granted them legal protections and non-profit-making agencies such as API–COLF and ACLI–COLF[18] assumed the role of intermediary. Particularly influential in this regard is the Salesian Order, in turn affiliated with API–COLF, the largest agency for domestic employment in Palermo, which works to gain fair wages and benefits for national and foreign *colf*. The early organization of the Filipino community owed much to the encouragement and legal services secured by key figures in the Order. The just compensation and decent working conditions enjoyed by most Filipino domestics continue to attest to their organizational presence. As the long-time head of the Filipino community told me: "We taught employers about our rights, and not the other way around." The extent of organization achieved by the Filipino community was an important moment in the move towards parity for foreign *colf*; unfortunately, it remains to be emulated by other groups, despite the continued efforts of the Salesians. In this regard it is interesting to note that the leader of the Filipino community prided herself on the distance she had maintained from the unions. Unlike "the Africans" and others, she pointed out, the Filipinos neither needed nor sought the attention of unions, but had quietly and efficiently protected their rights. She clearly regarded public protests as in bad taste and beneath the "manners" that set Filipinos apart from and above other immigrants.

Racist discourse, such as the stereotype of the sexually ravenous black woman, can interact with and be charged by much rawer forms of dominance. A high-ranking and Sicilian-born officer at the American Consulate, who circulates in high society in Palermo, tells of hearing views on race reminiscent of those of the American Deep South "a hundred years ago." He reports that among the *alta borghesia* it is the ultimate sign of sophistication to be served drinks by a member of another race, preferably clad in white gloves and uniform. Also, a doctor, who works in Albergheria and lives near the posh via della Libertà, contrasts the "true acceptance" of immigrants by working people with the hypocritical rhetoric of the affluent. Workers worry about immigrants threatening their work but accept them easily on an individual basis, as neighbors, for example. Among the bourgeoisie, who profess tolerance loudly, she has heard more than once "hard words" on the subject of sons' and daughters' dating immigrants.

The hierarchy of domestic workers presents another example of stereo-typing. More than one person explained this hierarchy to me in cultural and historical terms. Colonization, English in particular, so the theory goes, effectively trained whole populations in obedience to authority and in hard work, both virtues in the domestic servant. Thus the Filipino maid represents a pleasing synthesis of Oriental submission and Christian rectitude. In the case of Sri Lankans, this training makes even the men suitable for employment in the home; they willingly perform their tasks and constitute no threat to the honor of Sicilian husbands, being, as it were, eunuchs by virtue of their profession and nationality. By contrast, North Africans, like Sicilians, refuse to submit to authority and are not driven by a work ethic. It is unclear whether this is a result of improper colonization, cultural predispositions, or both. Such explanations illus-trate how labor-market relations can transform and charge racial and ethnic definitions of segments of the working class.

Conclusions

The bourgeois response to immigration described here illustrates what Wallerstein (1991) identifies as a central contradiction in capitalism between universalist and hierarchical ideologies and practices. By virtue of their position, members of this class typically support ideologies and (some) practices associated with universalism – democracy, meritocracy, and so on – which in fact explain and justify their dominance. At the same time, they themselves are the greatest beneficiaries of the ethnic, racial, and gender hierarchies that exclude many people from similar privileges. In Palermo, this class often expresses the virtues of democracy and a Sicilian brand of tolerance towards immigrants while it earmarks immi-grants and local poor as servants. Like the architect who casually asked about the effect of immigration on "the little people," many bourgeois Palermitans regard the phenomenon of immigration with calm detach-ment.[19] As long as the social costs remain low, it provides them with an abundant supply of cheap and exotic servants.

For immigrants and working Palermitans this contradiction finds more painful expression. Both groups appeal to universalism to redress inequal-ity and injustice. Thus, the poor man in Albergheria claims the right to a job because Italy's constitution sanctifies the right of all to work, while the Cape Verdian woman laments that skin color relegates her to domestic work and prevents her from realizing her full potential. Of course, both know from hard experience that appeals to ideals result in precious little. The Sicilian enters a competition for a job knowing that his recommendations are insufficient; only fools and the rich can afford to believe in ideals but, against his better judgment, he forces himself to make one more appeal. The immigrant regards the multicultural events sponsored by cultural associations and leftist parties as a sham and despairs of achieving real acceptance and significant earning power.

Worse still, as a measuring stick of human worth, an idealistic universalism justifies the inequality that structures success. Thus both immigrant and poor Sicilian, caught in the pincers of the contradiction, accept their subordination even as they reject it. Working-class Sicilians see the state as jailkeeper rather than guardian, denounce the collusion of mafia figures and politicians, and compare the integrity of their traditional culture favorably with bourgeois hypocrisy. Yet their seeming ineptitude in what is theoretically a fair game fosters resignation and self-hatred. The response of the immigrant is also contradictory. At the same time as they object to their lowly status on the labor market and their marginality in Italian society, they also embrace essentialist ideologies in an effort to set themselves and their like apart from other immigrants. This is why, late one night in a bar in Ballarò, a Tunisian man angry with "racism" in the West nevertheless, and in all seriousness, argued with a Ghanaian that he, the Tunisian, was not a mere "African" but something better – a westernized Arab. In the case of the Filipino community, members cherish their position atop the hierarchy of domestic workers while they express exasperation at being confined to working "not with our heads, but only with our hands." In a curious but characteristic living out of the contradiction, Filipinos attribute their success, relative to that of other immigrant groups, to hard work and education (an appeal to meritocracy) as well as to "manners" and a superior culture (an appeal to essentialist hierarchy).

4

The politics of race and immigration in the Italian north and south

The Sicilian thesis

In late January 1990, during the celebration of Carnival in Florence, about forty youths, masked and armed and calling themselves "avengers," beat several North Africans and a Slav. Chanting "get the Moroccan" and "sporchi spacciatori, tunisini di merda" ("dirty dealers, shitty Tunisians"), they chased immigrants, destroyed property, and clashed with police (*La Repubblica,* 1 March 1990). This brutal expedition to "clean up the city" was not an isolated incident. A week earlier, merchants in the historic center of Florence had sponsored a march to gain public support for their objections to the presence of unlicensed immigrant street vendors. Posters warned ominously of *giustizieri della notte*[1] ("avengers of the night") (*La Repubblica,* 1 March 1990). The neo-fascist party, the Italian Social Movement (MSI),[2] joined the march and led the chants of "rimandiamoli a casa" ("let's send them home") and "facciamo la giustizia da soli"[3] ("let's take justice into our own hands") (*La Repubblica,* 21 February 1990). The party's poster, depicting hands ripping apart a map of Florence, was plastered throughout the city. Although the party claimed the hands represented corruption, to observers they appeared significantly dark skinned.

From the vantage point of Palermo, these events, well publicized in the national media, prompted one to question why anti-immigrant violence and political mobilization had exploded in the prosperous north while the question of *razzismo* had remained muted in the impoverished south. Sicilians from all walks of life with whom I spoke tended to view the Florence episode – and similar ones to follow in other northern areas – as evidence of pervasive northern intolerance. One conversation stands out in particular. A few days before I left Sicily a priest introduced me to several historians from the University of Palermo. They listened intently as my friend described my research on Sicilian reactions to Africans and Asians in Palermo. As he finished, one professor took me aside and asked with noticeable anticipation whether I had found Sicilians racist. When I replied that on the contrary most expressed tolerance or apathy despite their worries about competition for jobs and services, she wheeled around to the group and exclaimed: "I knew it! We can't be racist because we've been emigrants for so long!"

These remarks, coming from a student of historical process, suggest the prevalence of preconceptions about Sicilian tolerance among Palermo's intelligentsia. In this view, Sicily's position at the crossroads of Mediterranean history and above all the experience of nearly a century of emigration explain the acceptance of immigrants there – or should justify such acceptance if it did not already exist. At the same time, this model contrasts the tolerance of the Italian south with the intolerance of the north. The historian referred to was in fact suggesting, somewhat optimistically, that the experience of stigmatization and marginality endured by Sicilian emigrants, particularly in the north of Italy, necessarily fosters a compassionate understanding for immigrants rather than a mean-spirited insistence that they should suffer as did the Sicilians. Her position further suggests that a fundamental intolerance in the northern Italian character explains current anti-immigrant violence and political mobilization there. This eagerness to compare oneself favorably with the north, to address and avenge unjust treatment and characterizations, is an example of the ongoing Sicilian reaction to anti-southernism in Italian politics and culture.

Using the Sicilian thesis as a starting point, I turned to media accounts and secondary sources to plot reactions to immigration among northerners and southerners. I found both similarities and differences, the most striking of which was the degree to which immigration issues had become politicized in the two areas. For example, anti-immigrant violence occurs throughout the country, but brutality takes the form of intimidating foreign workers in the south and exemplary beatings by neo-nazis and skinheads in the north. Similarly, Italian churches, unions, associations, and some politicians promote the tolerant integration of immigrants, but much more has been accomplished along these lines in the north. Finally, while many Italians express reservations and fears about immigration, political mobilization against immigrant rights and integration is concentrated in the north. I argue that the Florence events in fact marked the beginning of the development of the "new racism" in Italy.

These trends can best be understood with reference to regional differences in culture, economy, and politics. I suggest that the apolitical southern reaction stems from a patronage system that frustrates grassroots politics, the essentially non-competitive integration of immigrants into the job and housing markets, and an understanding born of the emigrant experience. The vigor of the pro-immigrant movement in the north derives from strong local traditions of political activity that privilege the notion of solidarity, often communist and socialist in character but also involving the Church. At the same time, recent political entrepreneurs, notably the Lombard League,[4] tap and cultivate the widespread discontent with an inefficient and corrupt central state. For these groups the important problems of the north are the result of the presence of southerners and immigrants.

I must stress at the outset that the following discussion is impressionistic, and the conclusions tentative. While the descriptions of Sicilian events are grounded in a year of fieldwork and interviews, the depiction of the northern response is built on media reports, secondary sources, and brief stays in Florence and Rome. Needless to say, a fuller analysis of regional variation awaits an ethnography conducted in the north. It is also important to underline that the analysis pertains to a specific time (1990) and places (especially Sicily, Florence, and Lombardy). Rather than laying claim to sweeping conclusions, my account's very specificity points to the need to examine variation in European reactions to immigration issues.

The use of the categories north and south also calls for qualification. Since the early years of Italian unification, the terms have led a double life. On the one hand, the ideological construction of the south as a "problem" to national development (Gramsci 1971) has served the interests of usually northern elites, from the Piedmontese state-builders of the late nineteenth century to the industrialists of the twentieth. On the other, the terms have also described, and will probably continue to do so for some time, vastly different realities. In broad strokes, northerners enjoy more services, participate more in political life, and benefit from a vigorous economy; southerners, despite rapid postwar change, battle against the forces of underdevelopment, a politically unresponsive state, and organized crime (for figures, see ISTAT 1990b). Use of the north–south dichotomy here reflects the conviction that these ongoing material differences are significant; it does not support or condone the image of the south as inherently problematic or inferior. That being said, it is also true that the terms are so broad as to obscure important convergences. In the past decade, for example, Italians everywhere have become increasingly frustrated with their local and national governments. The ongoing (1992–7) "clean hands" scandals in Milan, which have implicated the Socialist Party, as well as other parties, and figures in industry in large-scale bribery and kickback schemes, underline the dangers of erecting a dichotomy between the modern political culture of the north and the corruption of the south. Similarly, recent anti-mafia investigations have revealed the national penetration of organized crime and its links to high-ranking political figures. With regard to immigrant–Italian interaction, there obviously exists variation within as well as between regions; and the variations may well prove to be the illuminating cases. These qualifications noted, I continue to employ the terms north–south as a convenient shorthand for what remain significantly different social, economic, and political realities. If the preceding analysis of working-class and bourgeois reactions is correct, it is to be expected that these two realities will shape the ways that Italians in the two areas react to immigrants, including the ways they give political expression to their views and actions. The following description, then, seeks not so much to provide answers as to identify important questions and themes for future inquiry. Given the increasing politicization of immigration and race throughout Europe, the trends in Italy certainly merit attention, however exploratory.

Institutions and associations
In this section I discuss the formation of pro-immigrant political and other activity in Italy. Owing to the nature of the study, my discussion addresses the Sicilian context before comparing activity with selected areas in the north. I begin this review of north–south differences with a survey of pro-immigrant political activity for several reasons. Pro-immigrant activity is interesting and important in its own right; in point of fact, it dominated the early Italian debate. In addition, because pro- and anti-immigrant politics do not stand in isolation, but work off each other, an understanding of the pro-immigrant position sheds light on the counterposition, as we shall see.

At the time of my research immigration stood near the top of the country's political agenda. While several years later the press would be occupied with the ramifications of the "kickback city" (*tangentopoli*) scandals unfolding in Milan, in 1990 immigration made the front page on a regular basis. Across the country leading cultural figures, usually associated with the center-left and the Church, together with a few politicians, called for responsible immigration legislation. They denounced the state's contradictory practice of allowing continued immigration, while in effect denying most newcomers access to legal status and protections. For some, this practice amounted to a form of *razzismo*, tacitly encouraging the exploitation of vulnerable foreigners, and creating a situation of crisis in which immigrants were seen as threatening. Media sensationalism exploited themes of crisis and conflict, while also serving to shake people out of the languor of the self-satisfied myth of Italian tolerance (Manconi 1990; Marletti 1989). In the media, at rallies and conferences, the pro-immigrant lobby called for legislation that would regulate immigration and grant foreigners a measure of dignity. In 1990, their efforts helped pass the "Martelli law" described in the first chapter.

Across the country, hundreds of institutions[5] and associations waged the battle for immigrant rights and integration on other fronts as well (CENSIS 1990b; ISTAT 1995). These churches, unions, and political and cultural associations – occasionally aided by politicians – sought to aid immigrants with documentation and employment; provide shelter, basic health care, and language training; secure legislation and funding from local governments; and formulate and disseminate short-term solutions and cast long-term goals concerning tolerance and integration. Through their diverse activities, churches, unions, and associations contribute to the principal paradigmatic understandings of immigration and racism described in chapter 3. That is, they produce fairly coherent and sophisti-cated analyses of these phenomena, and relate them to certain guiding political ideologies. The paradigm of labor solidarity, for example, places the call for immigrant rights within the context of the rights and solidarity of labor (and citizens) as understood by the Italian left – a position sup-ported by the majority of institutions outside the Catholic (and Protestant) Church. To speak of paradigms and ideologies is not to suggest that all institutions and associations retain the services of full-time ideologues, although some do. Rather, I label as paradigmatic the under-standings they produce and disseminate, because they serve as models for both interpretation and action.

In general, early debate in Italy portrays immigration as more a resource than an insurmountable problem, and often alludes to the successes and mistakes of other countries. According to the prevalent discourse, this resource harbors the potential danger of a "war among the poor," the continued marginality of foreigners, and the specter of racism, if it is left unattended. Moreover, this discourse finds its expression in government and public arenas as a result of the activities of organizations and institu-tions. Immigrants themselves rarely enter these arenas, and when they do it is on the terms set by institutional frameworks (Danna 1989: 54), despite the concern for collaboration expressed by Italians. In this sense, then, there exists in Italy what Ralph Grillo (1985: 290), in his study of institutional responses to immigration in Lyon, France, called "the representation of problems and the problem of representation."

The recent date of debate in Italy may also account for Italian optimism regarding diversity, which has been expressed in terms of the contemporary idiom of "multiculturalism" rather than the earlier one of immigrant assimilation. The absence of any problematic fusion of colonial history and immigration in Italy, relative to the experience of many other European countries, is also pertinent in this regard. Fascist Italy's rather tenuous control over several countries in North and East Africa ended with World War II, and there has been no significant immigration from that area. By contrast, the sizable population of North African derivation in France, as well as the contested and political nature of its presence, stems from France's long colonial career in Morocco, Algeria, and Tunisia.

At the same time, this optimism derives from the process of dialectical representation so characteristic of politics. In broad terms, churches, unions, and associations define their goals in opposition to racism abroad, irresponsible government lethargy, anti-immigrant politicians, and racist currents within the populace. As a result of this continual battle of position, paradigms come to resemble each other. The border issue, debated as part of the 1990 law on immigration, is a good example. The center-right government proposed closing the borders and policing them with the aid of the army. The opposition, made up of churches, unions, associations, and non-governing parties on the left, in particular the Communist Party,[6] criticized the proposals as contributing to xenophobia by promoting a protectionist "Fortress Europe" syndrome. The left also argued that closing the borders was unrealistic, given the demographic trends behind immigration. Said Antonio Pizzinato, a long-time CGIL leader: "The barriers, the 'closed number' [*numero chiuso*], the 'programmed number' [*numero programmato*], are all excuses for those who have not understood the processes that are overwhelming our planet" (quoted in Cuffaro 1989: 14). Later, when the issue of borders was effectively settled, the Lombard League and MSI's call for the repeal of the law similarly served as a pivot of ideological opposition.

Pro-immigrant activity

There is a general division of labor in Italy among institutions and associations concerned with immigration. Here, churches excel at providing *prima accoglienza* (temporary food and shelter; literally, "initial reception"), unions call for enforcement of labor laws and enroll foreigners in their ranks, and associations publicize anti-racism and multiculturalism.

All press for government intervention.[7] Churches, unions, and associations typically espouse one or more of the paradigms of immigration discussed in the last chapter, especially those of religious and labor solidarity.

Until the 1990 law afforded many immigrants a measure of legal protection and security, no other institution in Italy did as much to relieve the daily misery of immigrants as the Catholic Church. By the early 1990s, the worldwide charitable organization Caritàs offered assistance to immigrants at over two hundred centers throughout Italy (Campani 1993: 514). In Rome, it conducted some of the first studies (e.g., Caritàs 1985; Caritàs diocesana and SIARES 1989; SIARES 1988). In 1990, it opened a large "polyfunctional" center in Palermo. And in the western town of Salemi, Caritàs restored part of an old convent for *prima accoglienza*, under the banner "know the immigrants to love them" ("conoscere gli immigrati per amarli") (*Giornale di Sicilia*, 28 July 1990; 12 October 1990). The most active representatives of the Catholic Church in Palermo are the Salesians; their Oratory Santa Chiara hosts a variety of immigrant initiatives, including a Tamil school[8] and the Social-Medical Center.[9] Don Naselli, the Salesian coordinator for immigrant programs, arranges masses in foreign languages, and coached the Filipino community into its singular organizational fitness. He also pushed for the establishment of a Palermo section of API–COLF, by far the largest employment service for domestic workers in the city. In addition to the work of the Salesians, the Chiesa Valdese (Presbyterian Church), helps immigrants find work, submit papers for residency and work permits, and get language training through its Centro Immigrazione (Immigration Center).

Despite differences in emphasis, resources, and sophistication, church programs reflect a broad and coherent understanding of immigration that I call the paradigm of religious solidarity. Christian love, religious tolerance, and the dignified integration of immigrants into a multicultural Italy underpin the paradigm, as I was reminded during Easter service at a parish church in Albergheria. The priest called for contributions for the Oratory Santa Chiara to aid "our brothers the immigrants of color." We placed money in an envelope stamped "Christ died that we might return to the Father and make peace among ourselves / AN OFFER OF SOLIDARITY FOR OUR IMMIGRANT BROTHERS."[10] Indeed, for some, immigrants conjure up an image of Christ himself. A priest, who had established a center for immigrants in the western town of Alcamo, echoed the Pope when he noted that Christ too was a foreigner.[11] Ecumenical in tone, this message of Christian love does not seek to convert but rather respects all religions as so many expressions of God.

Unions in Italy have played an important if not key role in calling attention to immigration, and prompting the government to examine and regulate the phenomenon. Like the churches, unions treat the question of immigration in many ways through various local branches, bureaucratic levels and divisions, and study centers. The focus of union concern has been the labor market: the effect of often undocumented foreign workers on indigenous workers and strategies to protect the gains of union workers through immigration legislation and the unionization of foreigners. Particularly significant have been the CGIL (Confederazione Generale Italiana del Lavoro), associated with the Italian Communist Party (PCI) and the Socialists (PSI); the CISL (Confederazione Italiana dei Sindacati Liberi), associated with the Christian Democrats (DC); and the UIL (Unione Italiana del Lavoro), associated with the PSI, the Social Democrats (PSDI – Partito Socialista Democratico Italiano), and the Republicans (PRI).

In Palermo, branches of all three unions have addressed immigration in a number of ways. Through protests, conferences,[12] and studies (e.g., ITAL–UIL 1989; Slama 1986), they sought the attention of the government and the public. They enrolled limited numbers of foreign workers, occasionally offered language and job-training courses, and helped those seeking to legalize their status under Law #39.[13] Also pertinent in this regard are two associations of religious orientation. ACLI–COLF and the associated Centro La Speranza (Hope Center) provide medical care, *colf* employment services, and other assistance to local poor and immigrants.[14] The Palermo branch of API–COLF serves as an employment and training center for foreign and domestic *colf*, affords legal services, and promotes the image and "spirituality" of the *colf*.[15]

The ideological bedrock of the unions' paradigm of labor solidarity is the notion of the rights of labor to fair compensation, benefits, dignity, and representation (this is allied, particularly in the democratic welfare state of Italy, to the notion of the rights of citizenship). As Ottaviano Del Turco, assistant secretary general of the CGIL noted in a round-table discussion, immigrant participation in the labor market is the "real point," lost, at times, in fuller discussions of tolerance and race relations (Pasquino 1989: 24). By calling for parity between Italians and foreigners, unions propose to move foreign workers out of a state of illegality (*clandestinità*), underwrite their dignity, and vouchsafe Italian jobs and the gains of the labor movement. Unions propose to effect parity principally through government or regulatory actions. On the home front this includes laws and policies to coordinate the entry of immigrants with the needs of the labor market, and the enforcement of labor laws.

Associations,[16] like unions, have played an important role in shaping government policy and tend to express the paradigm of labor solidarity. A core of associations such as ARCI and Italia-razzismo, for example, organized the massive 7 October 1989 demonstration in Rome for the prompt enactment of immigration legislation. They also sponsored the First Annual National Antiracism Conference (8–10 December 1989) in Florence, where statements on the rights of women, children, immigrants, students, and prisoners were drafted (see Bassetti 1990: 87–95).

In Palermo, as in the rest of Italy, from the late 1980s many associations either turned some of their attention to immigration or constituted themselves around it. ARCI (Associazione Ricreativa Culturale Italiana – Italian Recreational and Cultural Association), the influential national organization affiliated with the Communist Party (PCI) and the Italian Socialist Party (PSI), opened offices throughout Italy for an organization staffed by foreigners and called CISM (Coordinamento Immigrati Sud del Mondo – Coalition for Immigrants from the South of the World). Its Palermo office works with government, other institutions, and immigrant groups to promote immigrant rights and multiculturalism. It also sponsors and takes part in conferences, debates, and cultural events such as the annual Festa dell'Unità. The Centro Informazione Sud–Sud (CISS – South-to-South Information Center), informally allied to the party Proletarian Democracy (DP), which is to the left of PCI, also publicizes the immigrant cause through conferences and study.

The Unione Siciliana Emigrati e Famiglie (USEF – Sicilian Union of Emigrants and Families) is an example of an organization formerly dedicated to emigration which now concerns itself with immigration. In the words of its director, USEF concentrates on making immigrants "active subjects" by facilitating their organization (it works mostly with Mauritians and Eritreans), and by pressing the region of Sicily for greater immigrants' rights, including the right to the vote in local elections. Ellai Illai (meaning "For a World without Frontiers" in Tamil) and the Meeting del Mediterraneo in Catania exemplify those associations for whom immigration constitutes the very *raison d'être*. The Meeting promotes religious dialogue between Islam and Christianity, and has conducted research on immigrants (e.g., Scidà 1990). Ellai Illai, centered in the Oratory Santa Chiara and working primarily, but not exclusively, with the Tamil community, initiated language courses, a newsletter, cultural fairs, and an ethnic restaurant in 1990.

Groups formed by immigrants have been slow to form and fast to dissolve, with the partial exceptions of the Filipino, Mauritian, and Tamil communities. The Filipino community first organized itself in 1979, as it sought to protect the rights of the Filipino *colf* in Palermo. While it is linked to a national association with elected representatives, its organization in Palermo currently is informal in nature, centering around religious attendance at Catholic Church activities and social events. The community head, who has served since its inception, reports that fellow Filipinos no longer bother to elect her; they simply come to her when a problem arises. According to a representative at ARCI, the Mauritian organization, the Associazione Mauriziana Immigrati Palermo (AMIP), is the most recent of a series of rapidly dissolving and reconstituting Mauritian immigrants' organizations. The AMIP sports fair held in September 1990, however, was efficiently run, and was also attended by Ghanaians, Cape Verdians, and Sri Lankans. Sri Lankans, who have only recently arrived in Palermo, have created the Coordinamento Tamil and established the Tamil school in the Oratory Santa Chiara, described earlier.[17]

Immigrant-focused associations in Sicily, like their numerous counterparts throughout the country, typically endorse the paradigm of labor solidarity. They too situate immigration in a global context, denounce racism and exploitation, and call for immigrant rights and diversity. Because their members come from the left of Italian political culture, they, like the unions, hold as central the fundamental rights of foreigners as workers and citizens. Perhaps more than the unions, they stress that rights should extend to all as citizens of the world. Moreover, unlike both the churches and the unions, these associations do not confront the daily problems of *extracomunitari* – health, housing, work, and maltreatment by the authorities – but rather focus on studying, organizing, and promoting immigration issues. As a result, their discourse tends to be more radical and abstract than that of other organizations, their plans and visions more sweeping. More than the other institutions, they identify racism as the main problem faced by foreigners, portray the foreign presence as a resource in every way, and propose the collaborative construction of a new Italy enriched by diversity and equality. For example, Senzaconfine (Without Borders), an association founded in Rome in 1989, calls itself a "place of multicolored encounter." In its commitment to immigrant rights, Senzaconfine sees itself contributing "to the solution of the great problems which bear on the relationship of the countries of the South to the countries of the North of the world; on peace, on nonviolence, on disarmament (even unilateral); and on a new conception of [our] relations with nature and the environment"[18] (Senzaconfine 1989: 2).

The aims of Ellai Illai in Palermo are somewhat more modest. A group of young Sicilians with experience of teaching Italian at Santa Chiara and expertise in leftist organization and politics founded the association in the

6. Immigrants. Spectators look on at the sports day for immigrants organized by the Mauritian Association of Palermo (AMIP).

summer of 1990. Like other "independent" groups, Ellai Illai declares itself affiliated with neither party nor sect. Rather, it aims through cultural and recreational activities to promote "the integration, on all levels, of *extracomunitari* (workers, students, etc.) in Italy, with respect to their cultures; [and] their acquisition of the economic, social, political, and cultural tools necessary to a free and dignified existence" (Ellai Illai (Palermo) 1990: 5).[19] The association stresses the collaborative nature of its endeavor: one of the founders told me their objective was to "plan together" with immigrants and not for them. Because of their work schedules, education, and familiarity with Italian political culture, however, the Sicilians tend to formulate policy and then consult Tamils and others. On one occasion I participated in a meeting on a proposed newsletter. The leader sternly criticized my suggestion that a page set aside for Tamils appear in English. Against my observation that educated Sri

Lankans are proud to know English (a language, furthermore, intelligible to other immigrants) he maintained that publication in Tamil was necessary for the cultural integrity of Sri Lankans. On the whole, perhaps because of the organizational skills of its members, Ellai Illai accomplished a lot during its first half year of activity: its cultural fairs were successes, its language courses well attended, and the trial run of an ethnic restaurant drew a full house of Palermo's progressive set.

Institutions and associations in Palermo work to promote immigrant rights and integration in different ways, with different resources and different constituencies. Common to their efforts, however, is the invocation of Sicilian history and culture that seeks to make more evocative their general calls for tolerance. On the occasion of the CGIL-sponsored march in protest at immigrant suffering, representatives of the Communist Party inveighed against "fuochi razzisti estranei alle civili tradizioni dei siciliani" ("racist fires foreign to the civil traditions of the Sicilians") (*Giornale di Sicilia*, 15 November 1990). The theme of Sicilian tolerance, which figures prominently in much institutional and associational discourse, also illustrates the processes of ideology-making and representation. For many institutions and associations, Sicily's position at the crossroads of Mediterranean history and the defining experience of nearly a century of emigration explain current tolerance or constitute the moral basis for its enactment in the present. "We're almost Oriental in our disposition to hospitality," said Don Mele of Santa Chiara; moreover, he continued, Sicilians, in contrast to northerners, understand people who have to leave home to earn their bread. Echoing this sentiment, a CISS representative described how there exists between immigrants and poor Sicilians a "solidarity of the poor" based on shared poverty and the experience of emigration rather than some exalted notion of cultural exchange. This idea takes on a physical expression at the Presbyterian Church, where the Centro Immigrazione (Immigration Center) is replacing Associazione Siciliana Emigrati e Famiglia (Sicilian Association of Emigrants and Family), the Church's association dedicated to assisting Sicilian emigrants. The statement of intent of the Third World Reception Center (Centro Accoglienza Terzomondiali) in Alcamo neatly integrates the themes of a Sicilian model for tolerance and integration:

The presence of immigrant citizens and workers, in addition to constituting a real and objective problem for our society, also can and must be an opportunity for cultural and social enrichment in an area like our own – Sicily – which has always been throughout history a crossroads of diverse cultures and which has known, even in the recent past, the drama of emigration of necessity.

(*Centro Accoglienza Terzomondiali 1990*)

In this way, aspects of the Sicilian experience serve as a kind of moral and rhetorical point of reference, closer to people's perceived experiences than the heavy paradigmatic abstractions of multiculturalism as such. Not every institution accepts the notion of Sicilian tolerance or a Sicilian mission; indeed not even those institutions whose activity is centered around this theme do so when the need to solicit government intervention on a practical or legal basis is undeniable. However, the recurrence of the theme is a measure of its attraction and power.[20] Significantly, analogous formulations at the national level about the duty incumbent on Italy as a "country of emigration" do not enjoy similar purchase on the national conscience. The capacity of this Sicilian theme to give salience to more general and abstract formulations makes it attractive to institutional leaders who seek to communicate and persuade. In addition, it serves to distinguish the otherwise much-maligned Sicilian experience and to mark it off from that of other Italians, particularly that of northerners. As a union (CISL) representative asserted, "*we* can't be racist because the northerners are the ones who call us Africans."

By the ways and means already described, Sicilian institutions and associations have endeavored to make immigration a political issue. Have these efforts been effective or, as one associational representative suggested, merely a created vanity issue soon to be forgotten? Certainly, their work does shape public opinion, particularly among the well educated and monied. In terms of practical aid to immigrants, undoubtedly, churches here as elsewhere have done the most concrete work. The Social-Medical Center at Santa Chiara, for example, was among the first such centers in Italy, and API–COLF and ACLI–COLF provide jobs and services to large numbers of immigrant women. The work of associations, just beginning in 1990, remains limited. It is the opinion of most observers that the unions, in contrast to the churches, have done little more than talk. A CGIL representative admitted that immigration had caught all the major unions unawares, and that not before 1990 did they embark on a concerted effort to address the issue. Sicilian unions are weak and they face the problem of organizing foreigners with typically high rates of undocumented employment and illegal status. But their poor showing also derives from their understandable reluctance to antagonize their constituency in a context of weak and declining union power.

Significantly, institutions and associations pursue their initiatives in the vacuum of government inaction. Aside from the stray innovator in a local public-health office making use of a regional law financing health care for immigrants (e.g., De Stefano *et al.* 1989), and the opening of a mosque in

Palermo (*La Sicilia*, 22 September 1990), the regional government of Sicily has remained silent and inactive on the subject. The same could be said of the province and city of Palermo. Italo Tripi, head of the Palermo CGIL, characterized government lethargy this way:

The union [CGIL] is surely slow in approaching these themes [of immigrant conditions], but much more grave is the delay of local public institutions and the governing parties. With few exceptions, the parties currently show little interest in this reality, perhaps because they consider it without electoral benefit (at the moment since *extracomunitari* do not have the right to vote), without realizing the racist implications of such behavior.[21]   (*Giornale di Sicilia, 14 November 1990*)

His appraisal of political silence and government inaction could not be more accurate. The fringe leftist party, Proletarian Democracy, was the sole party in Palermo to make immigration an issue during the local elections in the spring of 1990. The city opened an Immigration Office in Albergheria in early 1990, only to close it several days later, presumably for lack of funds (Nina Rocca, personal communication). As of my departure in late 1990, the regional government had yet to present, let alone pass, legislation on immigration as required by Law #39. An exception to this torpor is a regional law authorizing health care to immigrants irrespective of employment status (Forti 1990: 115).

In contrast to the feeble if well-intentioned efforts of the Sicilian churches, unions, and associations, their counterparts in the north have succeeded in making immigration an issue of general political interest. Institutions and associations conduct innumerable programs, some of which have served as models for activities elsewhere. More importantly, regional, provincial, and communal governments have anticipated national legislation and established immigrant programs for temporary housing, professional training, health care, and cultural activities (Bassetti 1990: 99–102). The Florence of the Carnival violence (see p. 118) had hosted the first annual National Antiracism Conference only two months earlier. One member of the City Council, Moreno Biagioni (PCI), devoted his energies to immigration and opened an Immigration Office in May 1989 (*L'Unità*, 17 February 1990). The Province of Florence formed a special Council on the topic as early as 1988, and Law #12 of the Region of Tuscany provides for free health care (Bassetti 1990: 103–4; for details see Biagioni 1990; and Volpi 1990).

This concentration of political activity in favor of immigrants accounts for the quick and strong response in Florence to the events of the Carnival. Churches, unions, associations, and the local Communist Party in particular, condemned the violence as "racist," blaming the "undefended citizens"

7. Election poster. The poster, put up in Palermo by the far-left Proletarian Democracy party, was the only election poster I saw that dealt with immigration issues. It reads: "Against Racism. Vote D. P."

march for encouraging anti-immigrant sentiment if not actually inciting the attack itself. These pro-immigrant forces launched a broadside of media counterattack, demonstrations, marches – and political maneuvering in the case of the PCI's withdrawal of support for the Socialists in the City Council. Ultimately, they succeeded in defining the events, at least in key sectors of the national media, as intolerant if not "racist." Finally, they won the concession of piazza space for immigrant vendors, which was to serve as an example for other northern areas such as Livorno (*L'Unità*, 27 March 1990), competing with the alternative Florentine example of police sweeps and merchants' protests.

What lies behind the different abilities of northern and southern institutions and associations to politicize immigration issues? In admittedly broad terms, concern for *razzismo* in the north derives from a strong tradition of responsive local government. This is particularly true in the

"Red Belt" area of Tuscany, Umbria, and Emilia-Romagna, where communists have enjoyed power for most of the postwar period. Communist partisans played an important role in the liberation of central and northern Italy from the German Nazi and Italian Fascist forces, and emerged from the war experience with credibility and organizational skills. Excluded from national governments on ideological grounds during the Cold War, the communists distinguished themselves through responsible and far-sighted work in local and regional government. Today the cities and towns in this area are among the most prosperous and best run in Italy.[22] This means that there exist individuals, associations, and institutions, including governmental agencies, willing and able to tackle immigration issues. As of 1990, of the 383 *associazioni* working on behalf of immigrants, 334 were located in the center and north, with the highest figures in Lazio (71), Piedmont (54), Tuscany (49), and Emilia-Romagna (48) (ISTAT 1995: 47).

The tepid politicization of immigration in Palermo recalls postwar political experience of a different nature. As discussed in chapter 2, the city, and indeed much of the south, has witnessed corruption and the misuse of public monies on a massive scale, usually the work of a dominant Christian Democratic Party (DC) in collaboration with organized crime. *The Economist* (1993: 49) reported that the "interior ministry has already suspended 43 municipal councils in southern Italy, on the ground that they were Mafia-infiltrated." Despite recent challenges by the central government's anti-mafia commission and by the local anti-mafia movement, decades of systematic patronage have weakened the body politic. Whereas unions and the Socialist and Communist Parties form the core constituencies in much of the north, in Palermo and much of the south they are either weak or co-opted. This was dramatically evidenced by the union-led protests in favor of mafiosi and the construction jobs they represent during the 1986–7 maxi-trials in Palermo (Schneider and Schneider 1997). The presence of patronage also has a bearing on the feeble political efforts made concerning immigration. Immigrants, as the powerless poor without voting rights, are unable to offer politicians a motive for action; and unions and other institutions find themselves drifting in the vacuum of government inaction. It is no accident that the special Regional Council (*consulta*) on immigration has been ineffectual. Again, the nature of the state looms large in local political development; this becomes increasingly evident as we turn to discussion of anti-immigrant politics and violence in the north.

Anti-immigrant violence

The last three chapters have shown the related themes of southern tolerance and northern intolerance to hold a certain currency in Palermo. The concentration of relatively effective and well-publicized pro-immigrant activity in the north, however, casts some doubt over the Sicilian thesis. Review of anti-immigrant violence in Italy, as reported in several national and regional newspapers over the period February–November 1990[23] further complicates the Sicilian view.

In Florence, a historic center of Italian culture, the beating of foreigners during the Carnival ushered in a series of attacks. On several occasions members of the "Goebbels brigade" beat up North Africans (*La Repubblica*, 8 March 1990). Trailers owned by or provided for immigrants were burned (*L'Unità*, 30 March 1990), and there was also a failed attempt to run down four Senegalese with a car (*Giornale di Sicilia*, 27 July 1990). Other northern events included: beatings in Milan (*La Repubblica*, 20 March 1990), Turin (*Il Manifesto*, 21 March 1990), Varese (*La Repubblica*, 11/12 March 1990), Rome (*Il Manifesto*, 21 March 1990; *L'Unità*, 28 March 1990), and the Como area (*La Repubblica*, 2 November 1990); the shooting of immigrants in Udine and a series of threats to Italians who were bringing immigrants to a local church service (*La Repubblica*, 31 July 1990); the destruction of a trailer and the beating of one of its occupants in Milan (*Giornale di Sicilia*, 13 May 1990). Youths in Bologna threw Molotov cocktails at North Africans sleeping in their car (Cuffaro 1990b). Someone burned out a center for immigrants in Trento and left graffiti ("RISS") thought to stand for *Repubblica italiana senza stranieri*, or "Italian Republic without Foreigners" (*Il Manifesto*, 4 April 1990). Somalians living in Rome were told "qui i negri non li vogliamo" ("We don't want blacks here"), and found that their propane tanks had been set ablaze (*La Repubblica*, 13 September 1990). There was also the attack on a Nigerian soccer referee by disgruntled coaches, players, and fans on the occasion of a disputed call in a regional match near Pisa, and the subsequent burglary and ransacking of his apartment (*La Repubblica*, 7 November 1990).

Young men, typically employed and often members of skinhead, neo-nazi groups, or bands of soccer hooligans called *ultra*, committed the majority of these crimes. In Rome, police found notebooks containing descriptions of attacks carried out by "naziskins" (*L'Unità*, 28 March 1990). Police raids in Tuscany and Verona uncovered flyers, swastikas, and weapons belonging to the "Goebbels brigade" (*La Repubblica*, 8 March 1990). The Veneto section of the "Ku Klux Klan" claimed responsibility for letters sent to foreign (i.e., Third-World) students in Padua (*Giornale di Sicilia*, 25 April 1990). Smeared with feces, the letters began "Hello Dirty Negro," and closed with "If I'm a true Aryan I must kill a black man." As in other such slogans, alliteration and rhyme are employed: "Se un ariano vero devo ammazzare un uomo nero." These groups recall the heritage of Fascism and Nazism in their brutal attempts to "clean up the city," in the words of the Florentine "avengers" who chased and beat immigrants. Without doubt, they seek to shock and embarrass the complacent main-stream with their politically unacceptable extremism; but their acts are meant as exemplary, public corrections of a society they see as flawed, and are therefore profoundly political in nature.

Anti-immigrant violence in the south rarely exhibits an explicitly politi-cal character. Two Nigerians were robbed in Naples (*L'Unità*, 17 February 1990). In Sicily, the violence reported included: robberies in Palermo (*L'Ora*, 18 April 1990) and Salemi (*Giornale di Sicilia*, 3 October 1990); a rape (*Giornale di Sicilia*, 9 November 1990); the ejection of a Senegalese vendor from a public bus (*Giornale di Sicilia*, 8 March 1990); and the killing of an immigrant in the course of a café robbery (*Giornale di Sicilia*, 9 November 1990). Setting fire to an abandoned house in Syracuse in which several Tunisians were squatting was the sole example of politicized, northern-style violence. Police traced flyers distributed by the perpetrators of this event to a northern neo-nazi group calling itself "Ludwig" (*Giornale di Sicilia*, 20 April 1990).

Violence committed against immigrants in the south is characterized above all by brutal forms of labor coercion and exploitation, particularly in agricultural work. An extreme case is presented by the actions of the camorra, the Neapolitan version of organized crime, in the Caserta area north of Naples. Here, thousands of foreigners work the tomato harvest under terrible conditions, which include long hours, low wages, little and poor accommodation, hardened labor bosses, the threat of physical vio-lence, and local resentment. In addition to overseeing the harvest, the camorra occasionally enlists immigrants to transport drugs. When several African runners attempted to circumvent its control, the camorra killed them.[24] These murders were not based on nationalist or racist principles; rather they wanted to punish those who had stepped out of line and to warn others, both foreign and Italian, against similar acts of folly. According to observers in Palermo, it is a sign of the fundamental instability of the camorra that it entrusts responsibility to transient for-eigners (Alfonso Manocchio, personal communication). They say that the stable Sicilian mafia is biding its time for the formation of an established immigrant population whose marginality and stability will provide willing and trustworthy recruits.

Labor relations in Sicily exhibit a similar if less violent logic. Immigrants and their advocates describe as common the coercion and exploitation of foreign workers. The systematic abuse of vulnerable workers is not, however, confined to foreigners. Despite impressive postwar modernization, chronic underemployment and unemployment as high as 25 percent make many Sicilians vulnerable to the depredations of employers. As I noted in chapter 2, the most striking feature of the Palermo economy is the paucity and instability of employment. Thus a CISL union representative with whom I spoke cautions immigrants against interpreting overwork and underpay as expressions of racism. The exploitation of workers, she points out, is the unfortunate norm at the bottom of the labor market.

Carnival in Florence

While violence against foreigners occurs throughout the country, anti-immigrant political protest is confined to the north. More than any other incident in the period under review the events of the Carnival in Florence illustrate the intense politicization of immigration in the north.[25] I will argue that this signaled the formation of the new racism in Italy. The opening pages of this chapter present the events, which centered on the attack against immigrants by a large group of armed and costumed youth who called themselves "avengers of the night" and who vowed to "clean up the city" by kicking out the foreigners. A week earlier merchants had led some 4,000 Florentines in protest at the presence of immigrant street vendors. Marching under the euphemistic banner "cittadini indefesi" ("undefended citizens"), they had attributed to foreigners "la violenza, il degrado e lo spaccio di droga" ("violence, degradation, and drug dealing") (*La Repubblica*, 21 February 1990).

The attack and march provoked a political maelstrom, often centering on the charged question of *razzismo*. While none of the participants explicitly defined the term, they used it to mean hostility, violence, and intolerance directed against culturally and physically different peoples. The investigating magistrate called the attack premeditated and "racist," and suggested that the merchants' march condoned the violence. The police forces, on the other hand, denied any racism, calling the attack "normale teppismo" ("normal hooliganism") (*La Repubblica*, 1 March 1990), and began clearing the city of immigrant vendors with the approval of the Socialist mayor, Giorgio Morales. The mayor, when asked by a journalist whether "Florence had become racist," replied: "No, Florence is not racist. But there is a small fringe of intolerant people" (*La Repubblica*, 1 March 1990). Likewise, the local newspaper, *La Nazione*, carefully excluded *razzismo* from its coverage of the attack – entitled "Notte di violenza e di follia" ("Night of Violence and Madness") – and gave equal space to an article about North Africans headlined, "Droga, fiamme e vendetta fra neri" ("Drugs, Flames, and Vendettas Among Blacks") (*La Nazione*, 28 February 1990).

In response to the police sweep of immigrants, the Communist Party denounced the action as worthy of the old South Africa and withdrew from the City Council in an attempt to force the mayor's resignation. The CGIL, Christian Democratic (DC), Republican (PRI), and Communist (PCI) parties condemned the attack as an expression of *razzismo*, as did major dailies such as *La Repubblica*. Spokesmen for the Senegalese community denounced the march, which they had initially supported for its condemnation of drug dealing, as a thinly veiled attack on all immigrants. Students and mostly Senegalese immigrants then staged a hunger strike in protest at *razzismo*, to which the CGIL and, later, other unions acted as consultants. A group of sixty prominent Florentine intellectuals signed an "appeal against intolerance" and blamed the city's new-found infamy on its closed-minded *cultura bottegaia* ("shopkeeper mentality") (*L'Unità*, 20 March 1990). Attacks on immigrants continued throughout this period, with graffiti suggesting "lavoro agli italiani, botte agli africani" ("work for Italians, punches for Africans") (*La Repubblica*, 3 March 1990). One of the Carnival "avengers," who was caught by police and interviewed by the press, exacerbated tensions by saying that he was proud of what he had done and would do it again. He portrayed himself as defending young women and others from Tunisians, who he described as inveterate drug dealers, thieves, and rapists. International and national media coverage of the hunger strike and violence further embarrassed the beleaguered administration. As a compromise, the mayor designated some public market space for immigrant vendors; this ended the strike but sparked a brief counter protest by the merchants, who complained of "troppi regali agli immigrati" ("too many gifts to the immigrants") (*La Repubblica*, 18/19 March 1990).

These events catapulted Florence into the center of the debate then raging in Parliament as it passed immigration legislation. Parties opposed to Law #39 (the "Martelli law") – the League, the MSI, and the PRI – argued that the new law, by virtue of granting amnesty to all foreigners present in Italy before the end of 1989, had actually provoked a crisis, as exemplified by the regrettable events of the Carnival. According to these parties, the law did this by encouraging an influx of foreigners for which Italy was ill prepared and had no economic need; the law was also seen as provoking the justified anger of Italians at the immigrants and the state that were depriving them of their own resources. The PSI and the PCI, the sponsor and major supporter of the legislation respectively, countered that only the legal protections afforded immigrants by the new law could guarantee their humane treatment, protect them from violence and abuse (for example, that of the Carnival), and give Italians the assurance that immigration was at last firmly under the regulatory hand of the state. The PCI held a conference in Florence on Italy's multiracial future to emphasize its commitment to immigrant rights and integration. A large anti-racist rally, entitled "No al razzismo" ("No to Racism"), drew over 30,000 people and brought to a close the intense scrutiny of the city. In attendance were local students, representatives from nineteen immigrant communities, workers, and union representatives, as well as church figures, and delegations from hundreds of immigrant and Italian organizations throughout Italy. A conspicuously absent mayor Morales was attacked as passages were read from Martin Luther King, the Bible, and the Koran.

Parties opposed to the "Martelli law" used the momentum generated by the Carnival in Florence to step up the attacks on the newly established rights of immigrants. The Republicans (PRI) called for the immediate closing of the borders, while the MSI and Lombard League announced the intention – never realized, it turned out – to organize a referendum to repeal the legislation (*Giornale di Sicilia*, 6 September 1990; *L'Ora*, 21 May 1990). The Socialist and Communist Parties condemned these views as irresponsible election-year tactics likely to incite racism. The governing coalition of Christian Democrats, Socialists, Republicans, and Liberals (PLI – Partito Liberale Italiano), however, announced that it would close Italy's borders to most further immigration and take a hard line on illegal immigrants, which it did with unanticipated effectiveness.

Towards a new racism in Italy

Events in Florence transformed the politics of immigration and race in Italy in two key ways. First, the "Moroccan hunt" of the Carnival represented a novel fusion of violence and racial politics. Clara Gallini has pointed out how its brutality, occurring within the public ritual setting of the Carnival, effected the transformation into politics of a pre-existing repertoire of racial stereotypes embedded in travel brochures, arcade games, movies, and advertisements:

For the first time in Italy some people undertook to transform the "racial discourse" from the level of scenic metaphor to that of an immediate symbolic practice which involved the direct use of violence. As we have seen, a good part of the lexicon was there to use: it was enough to collect it, reactivate it and put it to use at a moment determined by political criteria. The strategy was therefore *political* as was the argument.   (*Gallini 1992: 217*)

Other violence visited on foreigners elsewhere in the north similarly draws on pre-existing models for excluding and terrorizing the Other. Young "skins" (skinheads) recall the lineage of Fascism and Nazism in their brutal attempts to "clean up" their cities and in their death threats to blacks as part of an "Aryan" duty. The number of "skins" is not large, however, and their actions are roundly condemned by all political parties. Perhaps their most important role in Italian debate is to act as a foil to the respectable parties who oppose immigrant rights. In this sense, their aberrant behavior contrasts with the responsibility of the establishment, and suggests that trouble inevitably accompanies immigration.

Second, by siding with the merchants and against the immigrants, the political parties opposed to immigration legislation legitimated the merchants' protest, which subsequently served as a model for mobilizations in other northern Italian cities, led, for example, by local representatives of the national merchants' association, Confederazione Generale del Commercio (Manconi 1990). Given this crucial national validation, business people could claim to be defending national economic interests and public order precisely through anti-immigrant initiatives. The protest, furthermore, illustrated that "an attitude of rejection towards foreigners need not necessarily call itself racist and should not be conflated with the semiclandestine violence of organized bands" (Manconi 1990: 59).

In the aftermath of the Florence Carnival, anti-immigrant protest spread and mutated in the north. Complaining of economic injustice, merchants in Turin, Milan, and elsewhere called for the removal of North African and Senegalese street vendors from central business districts (*Il Manifesto*, 4 April 1990, 21 March 1990; *La Repubblica*, 20 March 1990). Other mobilizations portrayed immigrants as dangerous and diseased. In Genoa, merchants, Eurodeputies of Le Pen's National Front, and local MSI members established a "Front for the Defense of the Rights of Italians." To facilitate reporting of the supposedly numerous and inevitable immigrant misdeeds, they proposed that a special telephone number be set up (*Giornale di Sicilia*, 9 March 1990). A pamphlet published by the Partito Autonomista (Autonomous Party) of Trento depicted immigrants as "carrying AIDS and drugs and being a source of insecurity and criminality" (European Parliament 1991: 33). The disease metaphor for immigration found fuller expression in the Tuscan town of Vada, where parents withdrew children from school in protest at the attendance by Senegalese immigrants at Italian-language evening courses in the elementary school. Parents claimed to be acting in the interest of their children, whose environment they sought to keep free from "malattie e pericolo" ("diseases and danger") – in other words, AIDS. Parents continued to object to the program even after all the Senegalese had undergone tests for the HIV virus (*Il Manifesto*, 4 April 1990; *La Repubblica*, 14 February 1990, 23 March 1990).

In this period, the Lombard League was also wont to describe immigrants as intrinsically problematic and incapable of assimilation (see, for example, *Il Venerdì di Repubblica*, 23 March 1990; *Avvenimenti*, 12 July 1989). Rapid cultural or ethnic change, warned League founder and leader Umberto Bossi, could lead to the development of "the pathological behaviors of homosexuality, juvenile delinquency, drugs, [and] create the psychological conditions that favor for example sterility [in the traumatized northern population]" (cited in Manconi 1990: 99). League leaders dismissed the frequent charges of racism in several ways. In a rhetorical move also favored by the MSI and Le Pen in France, LL spokespersons decried immigration as harmful to both sender and receiver societies. In one phrasing, it was asserted that "to bring Blacks here is slavery" ("Portare qui da noi i neri e schiavismo") (*L'Ora*, 21 May 1990). In the words of Luigi Moretti: "Immigration is a crime, for those who do it and for those who endure it [the presence of immigrants]" ("Immigrazione e un crimine, per chi fa e per chi la subisce") (*Avvenimenti*, 12 July 1989: 14–16). This pseudo-moralism feigns distress at the suffering of immigrants at the same time as it marks them as different and dangerous, and deflects the question of racism by identifying government irresponsibility as the root of the problem. The LL further claimed to act as a mouthpiece for citizens justifiably outraged at the state's encouragement of massive immigration at a time of increasing economic insecurity.

Protests aimed at the plans of local governments to house immigrants temporarily in north-east Milan illustrate the themes already discussed (*La Repubblica*, 7 February 1990). Advised and organized by the LL, protestors typically anticipated media claims of racism by blaming government irresponsibility for their own anger at the presence of immigrants as well as for the suffering of the newcomers themselves. Unfailingly, they trained their protest on the state by contrasting government inaction on behalf of its own people with what they portrayed as its unfair solicitude for the needs of foreigners. At a neighborhood meeting attended by representatives from the city, a man addressed the issue of racism and responsibility:

They have called us supporters of apartheid, but it isn't true: we don't want immigrants to be in a ghetto, camped out next to our houses and our children. . . . The tent city [the proposed temporary housing] is the symbol not of our, but of your, racism.[26]   (*La Repubblica*, 7 February 1990)

Warming to the question of children, a woman asserted to the city officials that "You don't have children, otherwise you'd be here with us" ("Tu non hai figli, altrimenti saresti qui con noi"). Another protestor rejected immigrants as culturally inferior and different: "We want Milan European, not a city of camels" ("Noi vogliamo Milano europea, non una città di camelli") (*La Repubblica*, 7 February 1990). Still another described Islam as intolerant of other religions. Like Bossi, the protestors define immigration as problematic, and hold the government responsible for the inevitable problems thought to accompany cultural mixing.

In short, the Carnival signaled the formation of anti-immigrant politics in Italy. Like the new racism elsewhere in western Europe, this new form of political mobilization shields itself from charges of racism by denouncing the violence of groups like the "avengers of the night" as racist. To obviate charges of racism it phrases opposition to foreigners in terms of such seemingly irreproachable themes as law and order, government irresponsibility, defense of local economic interests, and taxpayers' rights. It also tacitly condones popular hostility to immigrants by depicting it as the natural response of people protecting their territories. Yet intrinsic to much of this protest is the idea that immigrants are culturally inferior, if not diseased. Thus the unrepentant Carnival "avenger" sought to teach Tunisians a lesson with the aid of a baseball bat; parents in Vada attempted to restrict from the school Senegalese, who are assumed to bear horrible diseases; and Milanese parents feared the proposed encampment of fanatical Muslims next to their houses and children.

Because they reject violence and overt racism, and because they engage such resonant themes as the role of the state, such arguments emerged in 1990 as the most acceptable and widespread form of anti-immigrant politics in the north. It is important to underline that anti-immigrant politics are only now forming in Italy, and that their future direction remains uncertain.

Conclusions

The foregoing description suggests that it is the degree to which anti-immigrant fears gain political expression, more than a simple measure of violence or exploitation *per se*, that distinguishes what some Sicilians would like to see as characteristically northern intolerance. In the remaining pages I shall address the causes of this uneven politicization.

Southerners, like northerners, distrust the state as hostile to their interests, and not a few fret that immigrants might receive the government attention they deserve but cannot get. In particular, the poor worry about competing with immigrants for jobs; and some have done violence to and exploited immigrants. Yet southerners – especially the Sicilians whom I observed – have offered no support to League-style politics, nor has any local politician shown any inclination to exploit such fears for electoral gain. Two factors seem pertinent to this state of affairs. First, the essentially non-competitive integration of Africans and Asians into the bottom of the segmented labor and housing markets does not appear as a threat to most Sicilians. Bourgeois Palermitans freely utilize some foreigners as domestic servants, while the working classes oscillate between feelings of empathy and fear of competition. Second, notwithstanding the recent gains of the anti-mafia movement, the emphasis of the patronage system on the distribution of spoils among individuals and shifting coalitions thwarts grassroots political activity. Politicians have nothing to gain from helping or promising to help foreigners without the right to vote or even legal status. They also have little interest in mobilizing the masses, whose desperate situation is in important ways perpetuated by politicians' continued stranglehold over the public sector. In this patently anti-political environment, the politics of immigration is left to associations and institutions with little power; in this context, anti-immigrant violence grows out of a brutally exploitative labor market.

Northern anti-immigrant action and ideology, by contrast, took on a distinctively political cast in 1990, from the violence of the "Goebbels brigade" and other "naziskins" to the mobilizations of the MSI and the League. Several issues seem relevant to this trend. The first concerns the question of threat, and involves the integration of foreigners into northern society and economy. At first glance, the absorption of immigrant laborers would seem unproblematic. One of Europe's richest areas, northern Italy commonly experiences labor shortages and the call for immigrant labor is great, especially in services and small industry but increasingly in heavy industry. In fact, in the period under review, many foreigners registering at public employment offices in the north received job offers. Of the almost 15,000 immigrants who received jobs through the offices in the first two months of 1990, approximately 13,500 obtained them in the north (*La Repubblica*, 18/19 March 1990). For example, in Vicenza, 2,200 out of

2,800 foreigners obtained jobs, nearly all in industry (Forti 1990: 117). Attention to general trends may obscure important local variations such as the success, vexing to some Italians, of particular immigrant groups. Thus the large Chinese community in the Florence area frequently draws the ire of nearby residents and workers who complain that Chinese leatherworking activity takes jobs away from local Italian craftsmen and makes too much noise (Campani 1993). The situation is different in the center of Florence, where countless shops compete for tourist dollars, marks, and yen. The presence of African vendors selling cheap items is a nuisance more than a competitive threat to high-priced stores, although merchants attempt to cast themselves as the victims of government inaction because, they claim, immigrants who do not pay taxes enjoy freedoms that they as taxpayers do not.

The issue of threat clearly involves more than competition for work or space as such. In segmented labor markets, cultural and physical traits gain salience as populations come to be associated with particular kinds of work. As we saw earlier, Sicilians are just beginning to define some jobs as "fit" for Africans and Asians rather than for themselves. Labor-market segmentation has a longer history in the north, owing in large part to the postwar arrival of hundreds of thousands of southerners (Douglass 1983; Fofi 1964; Ginsborg 1990; Pellicciari 1970). Initially, southerners found undocumented work in construction, small firms, and services. In the notorious "cooperative system," southern labor bosses contracted fellow southerners out to firms at a fraction of the legal wage, then extracted their own substantial fee. Immigrants labored in a precarious state of illegality by virtue of a law dating from the Fascist period designed to impede internal migration. Even after the repeal of the law in 1961, discriminatory hiring practices ensured that southerners would remain at the bottom of the job market. Only in the late 1960s did large firms such as Fiat and Olivetti consent to hire southerners.

A number of problems accompanied economic subordination. Advertisements for rental properties sometimes specified that southerners need not apply. Many southerners were confined to overpriced and cramped quarters in downtown Turin, and the miserable shantytowns called *coree* on the periphery of Milan. Moreover, contemporary debate and newspaper commentary promoted an anti-southern ideology, which was encapsulated in the common use of the terms *terroni* and "Africans" for southerners. The derisive *terrone* stereotype endures today despite – and perhaps because of – the advances of southerners in the north (Colucci *et al.* 1989). Soccer fans in Milan deride the supporters of the rival team from Naples as *cani-bastardi* ("bastard dogs") and complain that "lo smog e il napoletano inquinano Milano" ("smog and the Neapolitan pollute Milan") (*La Repubblica*, 13 February 1990).

Many current portrayals of Africans and Asians as dangerous harbingers of instability may be traced to this template of anti-southernism. Thus graffiti in the north reads "Out with *terroni* and Bedouins" (Bocca 1988). Researchers found youth in Pavia intolerant of southerners and foreigners, as evidenced by opinion polls and graffiti suggesting "negri ni, terroni no" ("neither blacks, nor *terroni*") (*Panorama*, 28 January 1990). Targets of skinhead violence and propaganda are immigrants and southerners alike, as well as Jews and gypsies on occasion. For example, the "Goebbels brigade" distributed flyers inciting violence against Jews and *terroni* (*La Repubblica*, 8 March 1990); and "Naziskin" notebooks confiscated by police in Rome describe thrashings of gypsies, immigrants, and Italians with southern accents (*L'Unità*, 28 March 1990). Furthermore, the Lombard League identifies the "southernist state" as a plague far worse than the lamentable "africanization" visited by foreigners on northern cities (Manconi 1990).

Like the southerners before them, immigrants take the jobs that locals refuse, are made vulnerable by their precarious legal status, are relegated to the worst housing, and are seen as problematic and threatening to northern society. The Italian situation recalls historical patterns of nativism in Europe and the United States (Higham 1955; Noiriel 1988; Saxton 1987; Schor 1985). Nativists typically claim that immigrants are dirty and prone to criminality; that they are culturally backward and refuse to adopt to local ways; that they steal work and act as strike-breakers; that their allegiances are to foreign governments and religions; and that they receive special treatment from the government to the detriment of native-born citizens. Such views typically produce and reflect diverse anti-immigrant efforts, including restrictive legislation, discrimination, and violence.

While patterns of anti-immigrant discourse and practice in the Italian north suggest parallels between the experiences of southerners and Third-World immigrants, important differences of context are noteworthy. Both populations entered the bottom of segmented labor markets, but the labor markets and manner of their insertion were different. Southerners often entered northern society through salaried employment and union membership; as Italian citizens, they benefitted from political rights and social services. By contrast, recent immigrants most frequently find non-unionized and insecure employment in the service sector; lacking the right to

vote, they are effectively devoid of political representation; and as foreigners they suffer restricted access to social services. In a word, immigrants in
Italy – as in France, England, and elsewhere – are not entering into the relatively secure working-class structures that flourished for much of the
postwar period and that are currently falling apart under the pressure of
political–economic trends. Immigrants find work easily but experience difficulty in locating housing, obtaining medical care, and gaining documentation.

Thus, circumstances conspire to impede the stable insertion of immigrants into the fabric of local life. This rootlessness, combined with gener-
alized fears of racialized Others, can give rise to images of disorder and
danger. The period in question, moreover, saw a sometimes chaotic registration of immigrants under the new law. Newspapers such as *La Nazione*
of Florence did not hesitate to publicize crimes committed by foreigners
(e.g., 15, 19, and 28 February 1990). Housing scarcity was also a key issue.
In Vicenza, more than 200 foreign workers in possession of permits and
jobs squatted in the train station for want of housing (*Il Manifesto*, 11
May 1990). High rents, housing shortages, and the reluctance of northern
Italians to rent to foreigners created a homeless immigrant population. In
Florence, a newspaper poll found that many Florentines refused to rent to
"blacks" or overcharged them by as much as 50 percent (*La Gazzetta*, 2
March 1990). Some 200 Nigerians squatted in the former Institute for the
Blind in Padua, for example, while over 100 immigrants occupied a former
factory in Bologna, and 500 occupied unused buildings in Milan (Cuffaro
1990a, 1990b). The former Pantanella factory in Rome attracted perhaps
the most attention, when fights broke out between the over 2,000 North
African and Asian squatters (*La Repubblica*, 6 November 1990); the
factory was eventually destroyed by fire (*Il Manifesto*, 13 November 1990).
Such terrible housing conditions led to protests. When the city government
of Milan decided to stop providing lodging for a group of Egyptians
(which it had removed earlier from so-called "minimal housing" or *case
minime*) because it had rejected their request for public housing, the immigrants protested at the City Hall and clashed with police (*La Repubblica*, 8
November 1990). In Padua, over 1,000 immigrants and Italians gathered
to protest at the immigrant housing problem (Cuffaro 1990a, 1990b). In
Bologna, 400 North Africans occupied two public-housing buildings and
threatened a hunger strike if forced out by the city (*Il Manifesto*, 13
September 1990).

In short, immigrants appeared to constitute a kind of a crisis in the
north. Some responded with initiatives designed to integrate immigrants

into Italian society; others sought to cleanse the body politic through violence and overt racist ideology. Still others, notably the League and the MSI, sought to turn the public against those whom they regarded as dangerous and different. In a number of ways their appeals were aimed at the state. Etienne Balibar has suggested that the relationship of Europeans to the state stands at the heart of their relationship to "foreigners":

> In essence, modern racism is never simply a *"relationship to the Other"* based upon a perversion of cultural or sociological difference; it is a relationship to the Other *mediated by the intervention of the state.* Better still – and it is here that a fundamentally unconscious dimension needs to be conceptualized – it is as *a conflictual relationship to the state which is "lived" distortedly and "projected" as a relationship to the Other.*
> (*Balibar 1991c: 15*)

This quote illuminates the ways in which the LL and the MSI sought to rouse public opinion against public expenditures or the granting of rights to foreigners. In Milan, they distributed flyers against immigrants' seeking temporary shelter, reading "They have fooled you" ("Vi hanno imbrogliato") (Cuffaro 1990a: 22). Their appeals focused on the rights of nationals, the irresponsibility of the central state, and the cultural unsuitability of immigrants for eventual assimilation – always coupled with an explicit denial of racist motivation. In short, they attacked the idea of government spending on foreigners with the additional understanding that Africans and Asians do not merit integration. Like Le Pen's National Front in France, the League formally rejects racism and embraces the notion of cultural difference to such an extent that it looks fondly on the prospect of repatriating cultural Others so that both parties may retain the right of full cultural expression. The venom of the League is thus diluted in relation to foreigners; however, regarding the "southernist state" it is full blown. The terrain of fiscal and cultural regionalism has proved fertile ground in the Italian north, where the League owes its meteoric rise to a powerful fusion of anger at the state with a sense of local autonomy thought to be endangered by southerners and immigrants alike.

The politicization of immigration reveals the fragmented and contested nature of the Italian nation-state; and the fragmented nature of the state means that the us/them distinctions common to the reception of immigrants become locally based (Campani 1993). The Italian state is just over 100 years old and has achieved a fragile cultural unity. Italians capture the sense that their country is more a collection of cities and regions than a nation when they say that their nationalism is limited to cheering for the national team in international soccer competitions. In the past decade Italians have become increasingly disappointed with and distrustful of their political leaders and institutions. Eurobarometer polls for 1978–87 show that governments in Italy have enjoyed little support. An average of about 75 percent of Italians claimed to be "not at all satisfied" or "not very satisfied" with their government, versus 45 percent of the French and 22 percent of the Germans surveyed (Ginsborg 1990: 421). People are angered by the unresponsive bureaucracy and corruption.

This crisis finds different expression in the north and south. In the south, the integrity of the state is compromised by its inability or unwillingness to take control of its territory from organized crime. For this reason the anti-mafia movement demands that the state assert the transparent rule of law. Northerners, on the other hand, object to the state because it appears to take more resources than it gives back. The sentiment is widespread in the north but pointed in Lombardy, the financial capital of the country and the birthplace of the League. The League reflects this sentiment when it denounces the "thief state" and proposes to split Italy into a three federal states (North, Center, and South, with Rome to be left to its own devices). Greater control over local taxes and administration and perhaps the independent entry of the north into the European Union would all be expressions of the League's free-market philosophy. By fusing its often justified criticisms of the state with a virulent anti-southernism, the League has created a strident regionalism in which northern taxes and territorial integrity are imperiled by southerners. This ideology of exclusion, invasion, and blame has also created the conditions for the demonization of immigrants as parasites, unassimilable, and inferior. Unlike the National Front in France or the Republicans in Germany, however, the League's main interest is in the reform of the state rather than the dangers of foreigners *per se.* In essence, anti-immigrant politics in Italy has ridden on the coat-tails of anti-southernism.

5

Conclusions

Studies of postwar immigration reveal much about the causes and consequences of population movement for European societies, economies, and polities, and poignantly describe the often arduous life of the immigrants themselves. All but absent from this substantial body of research, however, is a concern with everyday European responses to immigrants. A similar lacuna prevails in many studies of race in the United States, and for similar reasons. From the late 1960s, the shift in focus from the "prejudice" of individual whites to the broader framework of "institutional" or "structural" racism generated powerful insights into the nature of inequality at the same time as, in important ways, it dismissed the questions of white racism, ambivalence, and anti-racism (Miles 1989: 50–6). Thus critical, often Marxian, analyses of race tend to attribute racism to systems, and ultimately to the elites who are thought to benefit from a divided workforce, and to overlook the actions of white workers in shaping their racial identity and protecting their own privileges. As a result, too many concerned scholars on both sides of the Atlantic take for granted how whites think about and act with regard to race and immigration, how they give or do not give political expression to notions of difference and similarity, and how class, culture, and gender shape views and practices. This oversight has obscured our understanding of the role of power, ideology, and everyday experience in contemporary societies. Fortunately, recent publications by, for example, David Roediger (1991) and Alexander Saxton (1990), in the United States, and Gérard Noiriel (1988) and Michel Wieviorka (1992), in France, show how research techniques common to the social sciences and history can be applied with success to these problems. In this work I have sought to shed some light on the dynamics of ideology and everyday life through an analysis of Sicilian and other Italian reactions to immigration, circa 1990.

Since it forms the centerpiece of this study, chapter 2 shows best the benefits of an in-depth investigation of everyday reactions to immigration. Intrigued by suggestions in the literature regarding the structural disposition of European workers to hostility towards foreign workers, I concentrated my efforts in Albergheria, a poor neighborhood in Palermo. Participant-observation, discussions, interviews, and questionnaire responses indicate that, despite their fears of competing with Africans and Asians for work, few working people express "working-class racism." In other words, few assert white superiority, denigrate immigrants, or blame them for the countless ills and indignities suffered by the poor and unemployed in Palermo. At the same time, exaggerated descriptions of the effect of immigrant employment and a deep-seated reluctance to see current immigration as the equal of Sicilian emigration belie a sense of European superiority. That Albergherians, in the context of material scarcity and the bitter recognition of their own marginality, refrain from indicting those even more vulnerable than themselves is surely remarkable.

Yet simply to declare them not racist or not very racist, whether out of class solidarity or apathy, is to ignore the benefits afforded by a closer reading of their ideas and experience. Rather than figuring as a footnote to the initial question – racist or not? – the idiom and intensity of working-class ambivalence towards Africans and Asians became the focus of the analysis. I propose that greater attention to the experiences, hopes, and fears of working people elsewhere in Europe (and the United States) will reveal analogous tensions in the reception of immigrants (and minorities). Workers elsewhere will not express ambivalence in the same terms as Sicilians do, nor will they necessarily hold their fear of competition and self-hatred in check with idioms of solidarity, as many working Palermitans seem to do. But they will often experience ambivalence and contradiction, because issues such as immigration and calls for equal treatment of minorities engage fundamental class insecurities under late capitalism.

Throughout this study I have drawn attention to the ways people, within specific cultural and political–economic contexts, employ an array of ideologies to situate themselves with regard to immigration and Italian society. Sicilian identity and experience, for example, strongly but differently inform the actions and ideas of working-class and bourgeois Palermitans. Working people rail at their oppressors in bureaucratic Rome and the rich north; they take grim satisfaction in reports of anti-immigrant violence and politics there, which expose, for them, the immorality of those who belittle them as *terroni*. The confluence of class and southern identity leads working people to see their African and Asian neighbors as merely additional proof of the injustice of the system. General western stereotypes of the miserable Third World, transmitted through popular culture and news reporting, facilitate this interpretation. But as the use of the term *tuichi* suggests, these stereotypes are activated primarily through local idioms and understandings.

The Sicilian context takes on a different meaning in bourgeois assessments of immigrants. The high-school and university students described in chapter 3, and in particular the local intelligentsia described in chapter 4, recall not only the emigrant experience but the history of Arab and Norman civilization in Sicily. In this way they would ground the integration of foreigners in historical precedent, and give local resonance to abstract formulations of anti-racism and diversity prominent in national debate. While willing to concede to northern critics the existence of local impediments to southern development such as the mafia, they too point to the concentration of anti-immigrant politics in the north by way of contrast to Sicilian tolerance. The majority of bourgeois Palermitans, however, do not occupy themselves with models for the integration of immigrants, although they too do not hesitate to take credit for a Sicilian brand of tolerance. Rather, they draw on existing representations of non-westerners to define foreign servants as fashionable additions to their homes and, in some cases, to theorize on the natural aptitudes of different immigrant groups. The fashion for Asian female domestics in Palermo (and, indeed, in all of Italy) thus grows out of the interaction of stereotype and employer–employee relations. The structural weakness of foreign workers, as seen in global patterns of inequality and their precarious legal status and economic vulnerability within Italy, facilitates and charges this representation.

The confluence of class and regional identities that inform Sicilian reactions to immigrants exemplifies what contemporary theorists have identified as the key to the power of race – namely, its ability to interact with other ideologies such as nationalism, sexism, and even meritocracy (Balibar 1991d; Miles 1989; Wallerstein 1991). Philip Cohen's assessment of the reaction to black-immigrant success by unemployed white youth in south London suggests the dynamics of ideological combination. The youths express a "*subordinate racism* which becomes 'commonsense' as a result of its articulation through a *dominant but non-racist ideology* of competitive individualism" (Cohen 1992: 93). Given the basic racist premise of white superiority, black success in what is assumed to be the objective meritocracy of the capitalist labor market must derive from an unfair advantage accorded to blacks rather than poor performance by whites. What is essential to note is that a powerful and satisfying, if insinuating and destructive, "commonsense" can and does emerge from a fusion of ideologies. This suggests that neither south Londoners nor working Palermitans are simply hoodwinked by an externally imposed set of falsehoods. Rather, using the means available to them, they seek to form explanations that accord with their experience and aspirations. This by no means excuses actions contrary to the worthy goals of equality and democracy; but it does mean that improved understanding of European reactions to immigrants – whether hostile, ambivalent, or supportive – must take into account the role of everyday experience and the interaction of ideologies within changing contexts of power.

Appendix

Questionnaire
The following is a translation of the questionnaire (originally in Italian), arranged by topic, given to the four samples discussed in chapters 2 and 3. I have divided it into four parts and given a descriptive title to each.

I Personal and employment information

1 Age_____ Sex_____ Education_____
2 Residence (quarter and street)_____
3 Are you presently:
  a unemployed___
  b employed occasionally___
  c employed full-time___
4 Is your employment status documented?
5 Are you a member of a union? If so, which?_____
6 Occupation of your:
  Father_____
  Mother_____
  Brother(s)_____
  Sister(s)_____
7 List the occupations of five of your friends.

II Race and other evaluations of immigrants

8 According to you, which of the following phenomena are responsible for the unemployment and lack of industry in Palermo? Place a "1" next to the most responsible, a "2" next to the next most responsible, and so on. ___Mafia, ___National government, ___Regional and city government, ___The global economy, ___Palermitans,___Immigrants.
9 Select a sentence:
  a ___A person's race is important and the white race is best; or
  b ___A person's race is unimportant.
10 It is probable that many immigrants will remain in Italy and marry Italians. What do you think of this?

11 According to you, immigrants are:
    a   ___More honest and industrious than Sicilians; or
    b   ___Dirty and dangerous; or
    c   ___Like Sicilians.
12 Among the immigrant population, are there some groups that are better or worse than others? Who and why?
13 Do you know an immigrant personally? How? From work, the neighborhood or other circumstances?

III The labor market and immigrant employment

14 Is there a lot of "black" work in Palermo? If so, who suffers and who benefits?
15 What jobs do immigrants have?
16 Do they suffer exploitation or intolerance? In what form?
17 If you were an employer, would you hire an immigrant? Why or why not?
18 What is the effect of immigrants on the labor market:
    a   ___They do not make a big difference because they take jobs refused by Sicilians; or
    b   ___They take work from us because they accept less pay.
19 If immigrants are paid little, who suffers and who benefits?

IV Emigrants and immigrants

20 Why did Sicilians emigrate to America, Germany, northern Italy?
21 What jobs did they hold in these places?
22 Did they suffer exploitation or intolerance? In what form?
23 Have Sicilians in the United States had problems living with other immigrant groups like the Irish, Puerto Ricans, Chinese, and blacks?
24 There are now in Palermo and throughout Italy immigrants from Africa and Asia. Why have they come?
25 Select a sentence:
    a   ___I agree with regulated immigration in Italy because 27 million Italians went abroad in search of work in this century, and therefore we have a responsibility towards other immigrants; or
    b   ___I do not agree with regulated immigration because immigrants pollute the white race; or
    c   ___I do not agree with regulated immigration because we do not have work ourselves.
26 Select a sentence:
    a   ___In the future immigrants will contribute to the development of Italy through their work, culture, and so on; or
    b   ___In the future immigrants will take resources and we will suffer as a consequence.
27 According to you, was the Italian state irresponsible with regard to its own citizens when it passed the "Martelli law" on immigration? Why?
28 According to you, is Sicilian emigration to the north and to America comparable to immigration from Africa and Asia? Why?

Notes

1 Introduction

1 The transition from emigration to immigration in Sicily is described by Caldo (1981), Crisantino (1992), Cusumano (1976), Guarrasi (1982a, 1982b), Rovelli (1978), Scidà (1990), and Slama (1986).

2 Undocumented work is very common throughout Italy and forms an important part of the sizable *economia sommersa*, the "submerged," or informal, economy, which by some estimates may make up over a quarter of Italy's gross national product (Paci 1982). Employers are willing to risk fines in order to avoid paying the state the taxes and other charges (for pension, unemployment, and medical insurance benefits) above and beyond the employee's wage, which itself can amount to as much as 50 percent of the wage. *Lavoro nero* covers a spectrum of arrangements in which none, part, or all of an employee's hours and/or wages are documented. Employees accept these arrangements to avoid paying additional taxes themselves or because they have no other option; in either case, present earnings are bought at the cost of long-term security (Blim 1990).

3 The term *Vu cumprà* is thought to derive from immigrants' mispronunciation of the phrase *vuoi comprare?* ("Do you want to buy?").

4 The full title is: "Urgent provisions regarding the political asylum, entry, and residence of non-EC nationals and the regularization of non-EC nationals and stateless persons already present in Italian territory." ("Norme urgenti in materia di asilo politico, ingresso e soggiorno dei cittadini extracomunitari e di regolarizzazione dei cittadini extracomunitari ed apolidi già presenti nel territorio dello stato".)

5 My description is consistent with the government's own. In a 1992 lecture at The Italian Academy for Advanced Studies in America at Columbia University, Minister of Emigration and Immigration Margherita Boniver plainly stated the state's goals and methods of managing immigration as a labor resource. As a sign of success, she noted that, as of 1992, there were 700,000 legal immigrants compared with 200,000 illegal ones; and that these documented workers were still needed, since 60 percent of the permits issued in 1990 had been reissued.

6 The Italian reads, "ricordo di aver sempre sentito dire, fin da quando ero bambina, che gli italiani 'sono immuni dal razzismo per natura.' 'L'Italia è stata fascista,' si diceva, 'per ignoranza, per conformismo, per paura, ma non è mai stata accecata dall'odio di razza.' 'Quanti italiani in Africa,' aggiungeva qualcuno, 'si sono accoppiati con ragazze nere, facendo pure dei figli.'"

7 *Oltre il razzismo: verso una società multirazziale e multiculturale.*

8 On 2 January 1991, the Italian Communist Party (PCI – Partito Comunista Italiano), rocked by events in eastern Europe, changed its name to the Democratic Party of the Left (PDS – Partito Democratico della Sinistra). In the course of the change a splinter group broke off, calling itself the Party of Communist Refounding or Partito della Rifondazione Comunista (PRC). In this study I follow standard practice and refer to the former PCI simply as the PDS.

9 The Northern League is an alliance, dominated by the former Lombard League, of regionalist parties or "leagues" from Lombardy, Liguria, Veneto, Piedmont, Emilia-Romagna, and Tuscany.

10 Mussolini was never convinced of the scientific basis for anti-Semitism in particular, but he put the racial laws to tactical use as an expression of solidarity with his more powerful German ally and as a means of scapegoating Jews in Italy (Mack Smith 1982; see also De Felice 1967). The relation of colonialism and the racial laws to the reception of immigrants in contemporary Italy has not, to my knowledge, been studied. There appears to be no direct ideological linkage, even in the anti-immigrant politics of the neo-fascist Italian Social Movement (MSI). Colonization was brutal but brief, never complete, and the Italian public did not receive the racial laws with enthusiasm. The heritage of the Fascist "blackshirts" was, moreover, repudiated during the final years of the war, as partisans liberated parts of northern Italy and the country ended the war on the allied side.

11 An exception is the collection of political cartoons first shown in Florence by the Cooperazione per lo Sviluppo dei Paesi Emergenti (Cooperation for the Development of Emerging Countries) (Cirillo 1990). In one, a smug conservative says: "These anti-racists are pathetic cowards: they don't have the courage of their base instincts."

12 "Invece che con l'esploratore nella pentola c'identifichiamo coi negri che ballano intorno per mangiarselo, ma rischiamo di mantenere permennemente intatta la rappresentazione della scena."

13 Notable exceptions include Essed (1991), Phizacklea and Miles (1979, 1980), Van Dijk (1987), and Wieviorka (1992).

2 When the bottom looks down: working-class views of immigrants in Palermo
I thank Gerald Sider for the chapter title.

1 Politicians and mafia figures are by no means synonymous with each other, nor do their interests always coincide, but the involvement of organized crime in the city administration and economy is beyond dispute, even if it is rarely open to conclusive documentation by virtue of its illicit nature. Judith Chubb (1982) chronicles mafia–DC collusion in great detail.

2 Notwithstanding these dilemmas, the anti-mafia movement remains the city's most significant political mobilization. After languishing for a period in the

early 1990s, the movement recaptured the imagination of many Sicilians, who have been impressed with the state's unprecedented if still sporadic crackdown on the mafia. As the ongoing "clean hands" scandal moves southward from Milan, it may well link up with the state's campaign against the mafia. In Palermo, the anti-mafia movement, backed by unprecedented support from the state, may in the near future create a second and more enduring "Palermo Spring."

3 ". . . hanno creato e salvaguardano uno 'spazio' *democratico* di iniziative culturali, economiche, sociali, ricreative da progettare e realizzare in totale e sincero *pluralismo*, convinti che le differenze confessionali ed ideologiche vadano accettate e gestite come occasioni di arricchimento e di complementarietà, piuttosto che di polemica e di separazione."

4 "Preferisco dare loro da mangiare un pezzo di pane, piuttosto che darle in moglie ai disoccupati del quartiere o ai raccoglitori di cartone."

5 Sicilian Americans use "eggplant" to denote blacks in derogatory fashion. A Palermo shopkeeper who had stayed briefly in New York told me the following story. A Sicilian emigrant, irritated at the declining value of his property, supposedly brought on by the entry of blacks into the neighborhood, would shout out "cornuto mianzane!" ("cuckold eggplant!") at his black neighbors. Another version of this theme is found in Spike Lee's film *Jungle Fever*, where Italian Americans in Bensonhurst refer to blacks as "moulees," the Sicilian American term for eggplant.

6 The number of respondents in a given sample may differ from question to question because not every respondent answered every question. Where respondents split their answers between, for example, two possible answers, I record 1/2 in each category of response.

7 Of course, such antagonisms did occur. See Higham (1955) on nativist movements hostile to putatively inferior immigrant groups such as Italians.

8 Currently known as the Northern League.

9 "Le donne lombarde . . . da sempre hanno trasmesso ai loro figli le tradizioni e la cultura lombarda basate sui nostri valori di: rispetto reciproco, onestà, laboriosità, altruismo ecc. Attualmente il nostro Stato centralista ad egemonia meridionale ha imposto in Lombardia il predominio della cultura del Sud in cui prevalgono purtroppo: furbizia, sopraffazione del più forte, arroganza, corruzione e spesso anche violenza. Nel calo delle nascite in Lombardia la Lega lombarda ravvisa il disagio di un popolo che sentendosi schiavo ha deciso di non più riprodursi."

10 Marco Jacquemet (personal communication) reports similar attitudes in Naples.

11 Giuseppe Sciortino (1993) similarly finds that workers in Emilia-Romagna see themselves as victims of labor-market pressures related to immigration, and see the government and organized crime as the beneficiaries; they also fear immigration could become a crisis because of government ineptitude.

3 The view from the top: bourgeois views of immigrants in Palermo

1 Currently named the Democratic Party of the Left (PDS – Partito Democratico della Sinistra).

2 As before, the total number of respondents within a given sample may differ from question to question because I report only those who answered any particular question fully. Where respondents split their answers I report their responses as fractions.

3 "Penso che sia bellissimo, spero che succeda il più presto possibile perché credo in una società multirazziale e multietnica in cui tutti sono eguali."

4 The majority of people in Albergheria (12 out of 15) and Zisa (35 out of 55) also see immigrants as basically the same as themselves. Working-class views are somewhat more negative on the whole: 10 out of 55 at the Garibaldi school in Zisa and 3 out of 15 in Albergheria view immigrants as "dirty and dangerous," while 10 out of 55 in Zisa, and none in Albergheria claim they are "more honest and industrious" than Sicilians.

5 Currently called the National Alliance.

6 By contrast, people in the working-class samples would weigh their decision to hire an immigrant in somewhat more economic terms. The 42 people in Zisa who would hire an immigrant say they would base their decision on the merits of the individuals, 9 on the fact that immigrants work for less, and 5 because they work better than Sicilians. Of the 12 in Albergheria who would hire an immigrant, 3 would do so because of the individual's qualities, 1 because immigrants work for less, and 1 because they are better workers.

7 These evaluations of emigrant life are far more negative than those offered by working people. Only one person each at the university and the high school judge the experience satisfactory, while nearly a quarter so describe it at Zisa (15 out of 55) and Albergheria (3 out of 14).

8 Currently called the Northern League.

9 "Non ne so molto. Immagino che subiscano i danni dell'economia occidentale che si sviluppa a livello planetario, distruggendo antichi equilibri, concentrando la richezza in zone limitate, depredando risorse naturali e umane dove può."

10 Among those at the Garibaldi school, by contrast, only a slim majority (27 out of 51) expressed such an optimistic view of potential immigrant contributions, although figures in Albergheria (8.5 out of 12) resemble other student samples.

11 At the school in Zisa, by contrast, only a third (14 out of 51) did not know about the law, although the high number of simple "yes" and "no" answers raises doubts about their grasp of its content (they had heard the law's name from teachers and from my classroom discussions).

12 The working-class opinions were more evenly split, with 15 out of 51 and 2.5 out of 11 disapproving, and 22 out of 51 and 4.5 approving, in Zisa and Albergheria respectively.

13 "I contesti politici, economici, sociali e culturali sono troppo diversi per unificare in un solo caso i due movimenti . . . L'unificazione dei due movimenti migratori la si può senz'altro considerare sul piano dei disagi, delle speranze e delle esperienze umane."

14 The CGIL is affiliated with the Italian Communist Party (PCI) and the Socialists (PSI).

15 The ARCI is affiliated with the PCI.

16 "Bisogna stare sempre in guardia. Quando vi attacca il diavolo? Lui lo sa che siete deboli. Voi forse penserete che vi può attaccare per quanto riguarda il sesso. Ma il diavolo lo sa che in questo campo siete deboli, nemmeno c'è bisogna che lui vi aiuti, si può peccare da soli."

17 "Le signore le vorrebbero per sempre, vorrebbero che non si sposassero, per non doversi abituare ad un'altra donna."

18 Associazione Professionale Italiana delle Collaboratrici Familiari and Associazioni Cristiane Lavoratori Italiani-Collaboratrici Familiari, described in chapter 2.

19 In his study of white racism in the United States, Wellman (1993) similarly found that middle-class people regard issues such as affirmative action as social issues, while working people regarded them as personal threats to their security and living standards.

4 The politics of race and immigration in the Italian north and south

1 The primary meaning of *giustizieri* is executioner.

2 Currently named the National Alliance.

3 The closely related phrase, *fare giustizia*, means to put to death.

4 Currently named the Northern League.

5 I use "institution" to refer to formations of historical and cultural significance, such as orders of the Catholic Church and trade unions.

6 Currently named the Democratic Party of the Left (PDS).

7 The categories of institutions and associations are not always mutually exclusive – for example, there are various Christian unions and *colf* agencies – but they do reflect a general pattern of who does what for immigrants in Italy.

8 Founded in 1990, the school offers instruction in Tamil, English, and Italian. The founders reason that by keeping their children abreast of the Sri Lankan curriculum the students will be able to resume their studies without difficulty when their families return to Sri Lanka after the civil war. At the dedication ceremony a Sicilian woman emphasized that Sicilians have a duty towards immigrants because Sicilian emigrant communities have asked, and continue to ask, for help from their hosts abroad.

9 In 1987, volunteers from the University of Palermo Medical School, aided by funds from the city, established the Center, described in chapter 2.

10 "Cristo è morto per riconciliarci col Padre e fra noi/UN'OFFERTA DI SOLIDARIETÀ PER I NOSTRI FRATELLI IMMIGRATI."

11 For a theological statement of this theme see the special edition of *Servitium* (1991), whose title, *Ero Straniero*, recalls Christ's Sermon on the Mount: "I was a foreigner and you took me in."

12 In June 1979, in Mazara del Vallo, the CGIL held a conference on the subject of: "Il mercato del lavoro e la presenza dei tunisini nella provincia di Trapani: problemi e proposte" ("The Labor Market and the Presence of Tunisians in the Province of Trapani: Problems and Proposals"). In May 1988, in Palermo, the UIL held a conference entitled: "Immigrati o nuovi cittadini?" ("Immigrants or New Citizens?").

13 The UIL entrusts its representation to ARIF (Associazione Regionale degli Immigrati e Famiglie – Regional Association of Immigrants and Families). In

1990, the Palermo police announced an investigation into the alleged sale by ARIF staff of false documents to immigrants registering for legal status (*Giornale di Sicilia*, 17, 18, and 19 October 1990).

14 ACLI (Associazioni Cristiane Lavoratori Italiani – Italian Christian Workers' Association) has long experience of safeguarding the rights of Italians working at home and abroad.

15 The Associazione Professionale Italiana delle Collaboratrici Familiari (Italian Professional Association of Family Helpers).

16 While "association" describes a specific legal status in Italy, I use the term loosely to group a variety of true associations, groups, and centers varying in size, influence, and affiliation that are united by their commitment to cultural and political analysis and criticism.

17 I noted little formal organizational activity among other immigrant groups. Cape Verdians, many of whom have been in Palermo for decades, have an informal network (Crisantino 1992). I heard little of an association for North Africans (UINA). Rather, many North Africans had gone to the Associazione Regionale degli Immigrati e Famiglie (associated with the union UIL) to receive help in registering with the police. There are also several associations for Islamic culture generally, such as the Istituto per la Diffusione della Cultura Araba e Siciliana (Institute for the Promotion of Arab and Sicilian Culture) and Al Farabi. It remains to be seen if North Africans and other Muslim immigrants, such as the Senegalese, will form a community around the mosque that was established in late 1990. The Associazione Culturale Islamica (Islamic Cultural Association) was established to run the mosque and serve as an umbrella organization for Muslims in Palermo (*L'Ora*, 7 November 1990).

18 ". . . alla soluzione dei grandi problemi che ineriscono al rapporto tra Paesi del Sud e Paesi del Nord del mondo, alla pace, alla nonviolenza, al disarmo anche unilaterale, ad una nuova concezione dei rapporti con la natura e l'ambiente."

19 "Lo scopo dell'associazione è quello di promuovere la integrazione, a tutti i livelli, di extracomunitari (lavoratori, studenti, ecc.) in Italia, nel rispetto delle loro culture d'origine; l'acquisizione agli stessi di strumenti economici, sociali, politici e culturali necessari per una esistenza libera e dignitosa."

20 The notion of Sicilian tolerance is allied to a more general sense of the island's role in the past and future of the Mediterranean basin. For example, the "Alliance for Progress" in Palermo offers cash prizes for the best student essays on the role of Sicily in current Mediterranean economic and social development (*Giornale di Sicilia*, 31 October 1990).

21 "Il sindacato arriva sicuramente con ritardo all'approccio con queste tematiche, ma ben più gravi sono i ritardi delle istituzioni locali e dei governanti. I partiti al momento con qualche rara eccezione, sono poco interessati verso questa realtà perché forse la considerano inutilizzabile sul piano elettorale (dal momento che gli extracomunitari non hanno diritto al voto), non cogliendo la carica di razzismo che c'è in questo atteggiamento."

22 David Kertzer (1980) describes Communist successes in Bologna from an anthropological point of view.

23 Among the newspapers consulted most frequently were: *Corriere della Sera*,

Giornale di Sicilia, Il Manifesto, La Nazione, L'Ora, La Repubblica, La Sicilia, and *L'Unità.*

24 This description draws from a number of newspaper accounts, including *Giornale di Sicilia* (25 April 1990) and *La Repubblica* (11, 26 April 1990, 5 May 1990, and 12/13 August 1990).

25 This account draws on my own observations and the following newspaper sources: *La Gazzetta* (2, 9 March 1990); *Il Manifesto* (21, 22 March 1990); *La Nazione* (19, 23 February 1990, 2 March 1990); *La Repubblica* (21 February 1990, 1, 3, 6, 8, 11/12, 13, 14, 16, 17, 18/19, 20, and 23 March 1990), *L'Unità* (3, 20, 27, and 28 March 1990).

26 "Ci hanno definito sostenitori dell'apartheid, ma non è vero: non vogliamo che gli immigrati stiano in un ghetto, accampati vicino alle nostre case e ai nostri figli . . . La tendopoli è il simbolo non del nostro, ma del vostro razzismo."

References

Amodio, Luigi. 1989. "Un'indagine sui giovani e il razzismo." *Democrazia e Diritto* 39(6): 373–85.

Anderson, Benedict. 1983. *Imagined Communities: Reflections on the Origin and Spread of Nationalism.* London: Verso.

Balbo, Laura. 1989. "L'antirazzismo facile." *Democrazia e Diritto* 39(6): 11–22.

——— 1990. "Vocabulario." In Laura Balbo and Luigi Manconi, eds., *I razzismi possibili*, pp. 13–44. Milan: Feltrinelli.

Balbo, Laura and Luigi Manconi. 1990. "L'associazione Italia-razzismo e la crescita dell'intolleranza." In Laura Balbo and Luigi Manconi, eds., *I razzismi possibili*, pp. 5–13. Milan: Feltrinelli.

Balibar, Etienne. 1991a [1988]. "Is There a 'Neo-Racism'?" In Etienne Balibar and Immanuel Wallerstein, *Race, Nation, Class: Ambiguous Identities*, pp. 17–28. New York: Verso.

——— 1991b. "Es Gibt Keinen Staat in Europa: Racism and Politics in Europe Today." *New Left Review* 186: 5–19.

——— 1991c [1988]. "Racism and Crisis." In Etienne Balibar and Immanuel Wallerstein, *Race, Nation, Class: Ambiguous Identities*, pp. 217–27. New York: Verso.

——— 1991d [1988]. "Racism and Nationalism." In Etienne Balibar and Immanuel Wallerstein, *Race, Nation, Class: Ambiguous Identities*, pp. 37–67. New York: Verso.

——— 1991e [1988]. "Class Racism." In Etienne Balibar and Immanuel Wallerstein, *Race, Nation, Class: Ambiguous Identities*, pp. 204–16. New York: Verso.

Banco di Sicilia. 1987. *Rapporto Palermo: materiali di ricerca.* Palermo: Banco di Sicilia.

Barker, Martin. 1981. *The New Racism.* London: Junction Books.

Barzun, Jacques. 1967 [1937]. *Race: A Study in Superstition.* Revised ed. New York: Harper & Row.

Bassetti, Maurizio, ed. 1990. *Razzismo e immigrazione in Italia.* Special issue of *Testimonianze* 33(3–4).

Belmonte, Thomas. 1989. *The Broken Fountain.* Second expanded edition. New York: Columbia University Press.

Berger, John and Jean Mohr. 1975. *A Seventh Man: Migrant Workers in Europe.* New York: Viking Press.

Biagioni, Moreno. 1990. "Immigrazione e razzismo a Firenze." In Maurizio Bassetti, ed., *Razzismo e immigrazione in Italia*, Special issue of *Testimonianze* 33(3–4): 110–18.

Blim, Michael. 1990. *Made in Italy: Small-Scale Industrialization and its Consequences.* New York: Praeger.

Bocca, Giorgio. 1988. *Gli italiani sono razzisti?* Milan: Garzanti.

Bohning, W. R. 1984. *Studies in International Labour Migration.* New York: St. Martin's Press.

Bonacich, Edna. 1972. "A Theory of Ethnic Antagonism: the Split Labor Market." *American Sociological Review* 37(5): 547–59.
   1979. "The Past, Present, and Future of Split Labor Market Theory." *Research in Race and Ethnic Relations*, vol. 1, pp. 17–64. Greenwich, CT: JAI Press.

Bonifazi, Corrado. 1992. "Italian Attitudes and Opinions towards Foreign Migrants and Migration Policies." *Studi Emigrazione* 29(105): 21–42.

Bonifazi, Corrado and Antonio Golini. 1989. "Gli italiani e l'immigrazione straniera: quadro di riferimento e risultati di un'indagine d'opinione." In Giovanni Cocchi, ed., *Stranieri in Italia; misure/materiali di ricerca dell'Istituto Cattaneo 20–21–22*, pp. 315–25. Bologna: Istituto Cattaneo.

Booth, Sally S. 1988. "Dove sono le donne?" *Labirinti* 1(4): 4–11.

Bourdieu, Pierre. 1984. *Distinction: A Social Critique of the Judgement of Taste.* Trans. R. Nice. Cambridge, MA: Harvard University Press.

Caldo, Costantino. 1981. *Immigrati Arabi in Sicilia.* Palermo: Eurostudio.

Calvanese, Francesco and Enrico Pugliese. 1988. "Emigration and Immigration in Italy: Recent Trends." *Labour* 2(3): 181–99.

Cammarota, Antonella. 1989. "L'atteggiamento dei giovani del sud d'Italia di fronte ai problemi dello sviluppo e dell'immigrazione." In Giovanni Cocchi, ed., *Stranieri in Italia: misure/materiali di ricerca dell'Istituto Cattaneo 20–21–22*, pp. 327–36. Bologna: Istituto Cattaneo.

Campani, Giovanna. 1993. "Immigration and Racism in Southern Europe: the Italian Case." *Ethnic and Racial Studies* 16(3): 507–35.

Caritàs diocesana. 1985. *Gli stranieri a Roma.* Rome: Caritàs diocesana.

Caritàs diocesana and SIARES (Società Italiana per le analisi e le ricerche economiche e socio-psicologiche). 1989. *Stranieri a Roma.* Rome: SIARES.

Castles, Stephen. 1984. *Here for Good: Western Europe's New Ethnic Minorities.* London: Pluto Press.

Castles, Stephen and Godula Kosack. 1985 [1973]. *Immigrant Workers and Class Structure in Western Europe.* Second edition. London: Oxford University Press.

Cavadi, Augusto. 1990. *Fare teologia a Palermo.* Palermo: Edizioni Augustinus.

Centre for Contemporary Cultural Studies (CCCS). 1982. *The Empire Strikes Back: Race and Racism in 70s Britain.* London: Hutchinson.

Centro Accoglienza Terzomondiali (Alcamo). 1990. Untitled press release.

Centro Sociale San Francesco Saverio (CSSS). 1990. "Indagine sul quartiere Albergheria." In Amelia Crisantino, *La città spugna*, pp. 259–78. Palermo: Centro siciliano di documentazione Giuseppe Impastato.
   nd. "Centro Sociale San Francesco Saverio in Albergheria." Palermo: CSSS.

Centro Studi Investimenti Sociali (CENSIS). 1990a. *Migrare ed accogliere: i percorsi differenziati dell'integrazione.* Indagine condotta dal CENSIS per conto della Presidenza del Consiglio dei Ministri. Rome: CENSIS.

1990b. *Immigrati e società italiana.* Indagine condotta dal CENSIS per conto della Presidenza del Consiglio dei Ministri. Rome: CENSIS.

Chubb, Judith. 1982. *Patronage, Power, and Poverty in Southern Italy.* Cambridge: Cambridge University Press.

Cirillo, Elisabetta. 1990. *Bianco su nero: satira e illustrazione su razzismo e antirazzismo.* Florence: Cooperazione per lo Sviluppo dei Paesi Emergenti (COSPE).

Cocchi, Giovanni, ed. 1989. *Stranieri in Italia: misure/materiali di ricerca dell'Istituto Cattaneo 20–21–22.* Bologna: Istituto Cattaneo.

Codevilla, Angelo. 1992. "A Second Italian Republic?" *Foreign Affairs* (Summer): 146–64.

Cohen, Philip. 1992. "'It's Racism What Dunnit': Hidden Narratives in Theories of Racism." In James Donald and Ali Rattansi, eds., *"Race", Culture and Difference*, pp. 62–103. London: Sage Publications with the Open University.

Colucci, Cestino, Paolo Segatti, and Marita Rampazi. 1989. "L'insofferenza verso lo straniero: indagine sugli studenti delle scuole superiori di Pavia." In Giovanni Cocchi, ed., *Stranieri in Italia: misure/materiali di ricerca dell'Istituto Cattaneo 20–21–22*, pp. 367–75. Bologna: Istituto Cattaneo.

Comunità di Sant'Egidio. 1989. *Stranieri nostri fratelli: verso una società multirazziale.* Brescia: Morcelliana.

Consiglio Nazionale dell'Economia e del Lavoro (CNEL). 1990. *Riconoscere e riconoscersi: il senso delle società locali e il vissuto dei soggetti migranti in dieci incontri territoriali da Como a Palermo.* Rome: CNEL.

Crisantino, Amelia. 1990. *La città spugna: Palermo nella ricerca sociologica.* Palermo: Centro siciliano di documentazione Giuseppe Impastato.

1992. *Ho trovato l'Occidente: storie di donne immigrate a Palermo.* Palermo: La Luna.

Cuffaro, Maria. 1989. "Immigrati di tutto il mondo unitevi." *Avvenimenti* (11 October 1989): 14–16.

1990a. "Se Ali cerca casa a Bologna." *Avvenimenti* (19 September): 20–7.

1990b. "Cittadini." *Avvenimenti* (10 October): 67.

Cusumano, Antonino. 1976. *Il ritorno infelice: i tunisini in Sicilia.* Palermo: Sellerio.

Danna, Abba. 1989. "Che fare contro il razzismo/scrive un immigrato." *Avvenimenti* (20 September): 54.

De Felice, Renzo. 1967. "La campagna razziale." In P. Alutri, F. Antonicelli, Paola Alatri, and Franco Antonicelli, eds., *Trent'anni di storia politica italiana, 1915–1945*, pp. 333–44. Turin: Edizione Rai.

De Stefano, Maria Luisa, Michela Messina, and Giovanni Pampanini. 1989. "Educarsi con gli immigrati." *Nuova Ipotesi* 4(1–3): 223–31.

Dolci, Danilo. 1959 [1956]. *Report from Palermo.* Trans. P. D. Cummins. New York: Viking.

Donald, James and Ali Rattansi, eds. 1992. *"Race", Culture and Difference.* London: Sage Publications with the Open University.

Douglass, William. 1983. "Migration in Italy." In Michael Kenny and David

Kertzer, eds., *Urban Life in Mediterranean Europe: Anthropological Perspectives*, pp. 162–202. Urbana, IL: University of Illinois Press.

The Economist. 1993. "Roots Go Deep." *The Economist* 326 (No. 7,794): 49.

Ellai Illai (Palermo). 1990. "Atto costitutivo di associazione." (25 June).

Essed, Philomena. 1991. *Understanding Everyday Racism: an Interdisciplinary Theory.* Newbury Park, CA: Sage Publications.

European Parliament. 1991. *Report Drawn up on Behalf of the Committee of Inquiry into Racism and Xenophobia.* Rapporteur, Glyn Ford. Brussels: Office for Official Publications of the European Communities.

Ferrarotti, Franco. 1989 [1988]. *Oltre il razzismo: verso la società multirazziale e multiculturale.* Second edition. Rome: Armando Editore.

Fofi, Goffredo. 1964. *L'immigrazione meridionale a Torino.* Milan: Feltrinelli.

Forti, Marina. 1990. "Inclusi, esclusi, semi-esclusi." In Laura Balbo and Luigi Manconi, eds., *I razzismi possibili*, pp. 105–22. Milan: Feltrinelli.

Fortunato, Mario and Salah Methnani. 1990. *Immigrato.* Rome–Naples: Edizioni Theoria.

Franchini, Roberto and Dario Guidi. 1993. *"Premesso che non sono razzista": l'opinione di mille modenesi sull'immigrazione extra-comunitaria.* Rome: Editori Riuniti.

Frigessi, Delia. 1989. "Alcuni stereotipi nell'Italia di oggi." *La Critica Sociologica* 89: 86–93.

Gallini, Clara. 1989. "Arabesque: immagini di un mito." *La Critica Sociologica* 89: 98–104.

1992. "Dangerous Games: Racism as Practised in Italian Popular Culture." *Cultural Studies* 6(2): 207–17.

Gallissot, René. 1989. "Is Europe Combining Two Forms of Racism?" *New Political Science* 16/17: 79–89.

Giardesco, Gianni. 1988. *Dai magliari ai vu cumprà.* Soveria Mannelli: Rubettino Editore.

Gilroy, Paul. 1987. *"There Ain't No Black in the Union Jack": the Cultural Politics of "Race" and Nation.* London: Hutchinson.

Ginsborg, Paul. 1990. *A History of Contemporary Italy: Society and Politics 1943–1988.* London: Penguin Books.

Gordon, David, Richard Edwards, and Michael Reich. 1982. *Segmented Work, Divided Workers: the Historical Transformation of Labor in the United States.* Cambridge: Cambridge University Press.

Gramsci, Antonio. 1971. *Selections from the Prison Notebooks of Antonio Gramsci.* Ed. and trans. Q. Hoare and G. N. Smith. New York: International Publishers.

Greenberg, Stanley. 1980. *Race and State in Capitalist Development: Comparative Perspectives.* New Haven, CT: Yale University Press.

Grillo, Ralph D. 1985. *Ideologies and Institutions in Urban France: the Representation of Immigrants.* Cambridge: Cambridge University Press.

Grimm, Reinhold and Jost Hermand, eds. 1986. *Blacks and German Culture.* Madison, WI: University of Wisconsin Press.

Guala, Chito. 1989 "Atteggiamenti verso gli immigrati del Terzo Mondo: una ricerca a Torino." In Giovanni Cocchi, ed., *Stranieri in Italia: misure/materiali di ricerca dell'Istituto Cattaneo 20–21–22*, pp. 391–402. Bologna: Istituto Cattaneo.

Guarrasi, Vincenzo. 1978. *La condizione marginale*. Palermo: Sellerio.

　1980. "Il quartiere 'tradizionale': marginalità e partecipazione." In Vieri Quilici, ed., *Palermo centro storico*, pp. 69–90. Rome: Officina Edizioni.

　1982a. "L'immigrazione straniera in Sicilia." In Vincenzo Guarrasi, ed., *Lavoratori stranieri in Sicilia*, pp. 1–49. Palermo: Centro Regionale Immigrati Stranieri.

　1982b. "Donna, emigrazione e società mediterranee: riflessioni sull'immigrazione familiare a Mazara del Vallo." In *Donna e società*, Atti del IV Congresso Internazionale di Studi Antropologi Siciliani, pp. 489–509. Palermo.

Guillaumin, Colette. 1995. *Racism, Sexism, Power and Ideology*. London: Routledge.

Hall, Stuart. 1980. "Race, Articulation and Societies Structured in Dominance." In *Sociological Theories: Race and Colonialism*, pp. 305–45. Paris: UNESCO.

　1986. "Gramsci's Relevance for the Study of Race and Ethnicity." *Journal of Communication Inquiries* 10: 5–27.

Hartmann, Paul and Charles Husband. 1974. *Racism and the Mass Media: a Study of the Role of the Mass Media in the Formation of White Beliefs and Attitudes in Britain*. London: Davis Poynter.

Higham, John. 1955. *Stangers in the Land: Patterns of American Nativism, 1869–1925*. New Brunswick, NJ: Rutgers University Press.

Husband, Charles, ed. 1987a. *"Race" in Britain: Continuity and Change*. London: Hutchinson.

　1987b. "Introduction." In Charles Husband, ed., *"Race" in Britain: Continuity and Change*, pp. 11–23. London: Hutchinson.

　1987c. "British Racisms: the Construction of Racial Ideologies." In Charles Husband, ed., *"Race" in Britain: Continuity and Change*, pp. 319–31. London: Hutchinson.

Husbands, Christopher. 1983. *Racial Exclusionism and the City: the Urban Support of the National Front*. London: George Allen & Unwin.

　1992. "The Other Face of 1992: the Extreme-Right Explosion in Western Europe." *Parliamentary Affairs* 45(3): 267–84.

ISTAT (Istituto Nazionale di Statistica). 1990a. *Gli immigrati presenti in Italia: una stima per l'anno 1989*. Prepared for the Conferenza Nazionale dell'Immigrazione. Rome: ISTAT.

　1990b. *Le regioni in cifre*. Rome: ISTAT.

　1995. *Gli immigrati in Italia: fonti statistiche*. Rome: ISTAT.

Italia-razzismo. 1990. *Gli Italiani e l'immagine dell'immigrato*. Rome: Italia–razzismo.

ITAL–UIL. 1989. *Il diritto di voto amministrativo agli immigrati extracomunitari in Italia*. Special issue of *Lavoro Italiano nel Mondo* 7(4).

Kertzer, David. 1980. *Comrades and Christians*. Cambridge: Cambridge University Press.

Khouma, Pap, with Oreste Pivetta. 1990. *Io, venditore di elefanti*. Milan: Garzanti.

King, Russell. 1993a. "European International Migration 1945–1990: a Statistical and Geographic Overview." In Russell King, ed., *Mass Migrations in Europe: the Legacy and the Future*, pp. 19–39. London: Belhaven Press.

　1993b. "Recent Immigration to Italy: Character, Causes and Consequences." *GeoJournal* 30(3): 283–92.

Leschiutta, Pier Paolo. 1989. "Il pregiudizio sornione." *La Critica Sociologica* 89: 105–11.

McDonogh, Gary. 1992. "The Face Behind the Door: European Integration, Immigration, and Identity." In Thomas Wilson, ed., *Cultural Change and the New Europe*, pp. 143–65. Newbury Park, CA: Sage Publications.

Macioti, Maria and Enrico Pugliese. 1991. *Gli immigrati in Italia*. Bari: Laterza.

Mack Smith, Denis. 1982. *Mussolini: a Biography*. New York: Knopf.

Manconi, Luigi. 1990. "Razzismo interno, razzismo esterno e strategia del chi c'è c'è." In Laura Balbo and Luigi Manconi, eds., *I razzismi possibili*, pp. 45–91. Milan: Feltrinelli.

Mansoubi, Mahmoud. 1990. *Noi stranieri d'Italia: immigrazione e mass media*. Lucca: Pacini Fazzi.

Mansueto, Serafino. 1989. "Immigrati a Palermo: l'esperienza del poliambulatorio di Santa Chiara." *Una Città per l'Uomo* 8(4–5): 18–23.

Maraini, Dacia. 1990. "Il popolo d'emigranti s'è scoperto razzista." *L'Unità* (8 March 1990): 8.

Marletti, Carlo. 1989. "Mass media e razzismo in Italia." *Democrazia e Diritto* 39(6): 107–26.

Melotti, Umberto. 1989. "L'immigrazione straniera in Italia: da caso anomalo a caso esemplare." In Giovanni Cocchi, ed., *Stranieri in Italia: misure/materiali di ricerca dell'Istituto Cattaneo 20–21–22*, pp. 31–43. Bologna: Istituto Cattaneo.

Miles, Robert. 1982. *Racism and Migrant Labour: a Critical Text*. London: Routledge & Kegan Paul.

1989. *Racism*. London: Routledge, Chapman & Hall.

1993. *Racism after "Race Relations"*. London: Routledge.

Miles, Robert and Victor Satzewich. 1990. "Migration, Racism and 'Postmodern' Capitalism." *Economy and Society* 19(3): 334–58.

Montanari, Armando and Antonio Cortese. 1993. "Third World Immigrants in Italy." In Russell King, ed., *Mass Migrations in Europe: the Legacy and the Future*, pp. 275–92. London: Belhaven Press.

Monticelli, Giuseppe. 1992. "Gli immigrati in Italia." *Affari Sociali Internazionali* 20(3): 63–80.

Mullings, Leith. 1978. "Ethnicity and Stratification in the Urban United States." *Annals of the New York Academy of Sciences* 318: 10–22.

Nascimbene, Bruno. 1990. "La legge e oltre la legge." In Laura Balbo and Luigi Manconi, eds., *I razzismi possibili*, pp. 123–39. Milan: Feltrinelli.

Noiriel, Gérard. 1988. *Le creuset français: histoire de l'immigration XIXᵉ–XXᵉ siècles*. Paris: Editions du Seuil.

Paci, M. 1982. *La struttura sociale italiana*. Bologna: Il Mulino.

Panorama. 28 January 1990.

Pasquino, Gianfranco. 1989 "Cinque domande sull'immigrazione extra-comunitaria in Italia." *Immigrati Non Cittadini* 1: 13–44.

Pellicciari, Giovanni, ed. 1970. *L'immigrazione nel triangolo industriale*. Milan: Franco Angeli

Phizacklea, Annie and Robert Miles. 1979. "Working-Class Racist Beliefs in the Inner City." In Robert Miles and Annie Phizacklea, eds., *Racism and Political Action in Britain*, pp. 93–123. London: Routledge & Kegan Paul.

1980. *Labour and Racism*. London: Routledge & Kegan Paul.

Piccoli, Italo. 1993. "La cultura del lavoro e la solidarietà: gli immigrati extracomunitari nei presidi della Lega Lombarda." In Marcella delle Donne, Umberto Melotti, and Stefano Petilli, eds., *Immigrazione in Europa*, pp. 397–406. Università degli studi di Roma La Sapienza-Dipartimento di Sociologia. Roma: Centro Europeo di Scienze Sociali (CEDISS).

Pitkin, Donald. 1985. *The House that Giacomo Built: History of an Italian Family, 1898–1978*. Cambridge: Cambridge University Press.

Poche, Bernard. 1991–2. "The Lombard League: From Cultural Autonomy to Integral Federalism." *Telos* 90: 71–81.

Poliakov, Leon. 1974. *The Aryan Myth: a History of Racist and Nationalist Ideas in Europe*. Trans. E. Howard. New York: Basic Books.

Portelli, Alessandro. 1989. "Su alcune forme e articolazioni del discorso razzista nella cultura di massa in Italia." *La Critica Sociologica* 89: 94–97.

Pugliese, Enrico. 1989. "L'immigrazione dei lavoratori in Italia." *Immigrati Non Cittadini* 1: 45–66.

   1991. "Le interpretazioni del razzismo nel dibattito italiano sulla immigrazione." *La Critica Sociologica* 99: 84–105.

   1993. "Restructuring of the Labour Market and the Role of Third World Migrations in Europe." *Environment, Planning, Development: Society and Space* 11: 513–22.

Quilici, Vieri, ed. 1980. *Palermo centro storico*. Rome: Officina Edizioni.

Raffaele, Giovanni. 1992. "Le immigrate extracomunitarie in Italia." *Studi Emigrazione* 29 (106): 194–225.

Rattansi, Ali. 1992. "Changing the Subject? Racism, Culture and Education." In James Donald and Ali Rattansi, eds., *"Race", Culture and Difference*, pp. 11–48. London: Sage Publications with the Open University.

Reeves, Frank. 1983. *British Racial Discourse: a Study of British Political Discourse about Race and Race-Related Matters*. Cambridge: Cambridge University Press.

Renda, Francesco. 1989 [1963]. *L'emigrazione in Sicilia, 1652–1961*. Aggiornamento di Eugenio Greco. Caltanissetta and Rome: Salvatore Sciascia Editore.

Roediger, David. 1991. *The Wages of Whiteness: Race and the Making of the American Working Class*. New York: Verso.

Rovelli, Roberto. 1978. "Le immigrazioni nord-africane (1968–1977) e la realtà socio-economica del trapanese." *Il Ponte* 5: 497–509.

Said, Edward. 1978. *Orientalism*. New York: Random House.

Saxton, Alexander. 1987 [1971]. *The Indispensable Enemy: Labor and the Anti-Chinese Movement in California*. Berkeley, CA: University of California Press.

   1990. *The Rise and Fall of the White Republic: Class Politics and Mass Culture in the Nineteenth Century*. London and New York: Verso.

Schmidt, Steffen W. ed. 1977. *Friends, Followers, and Factions: a Reader in Political Clientelism*. Berkeley, CA: University of California Press.

Schneider, Jane and Peter Schneider. 1976. *Culture and Political Economy of Western Sicily*. New York: Academic Press.

   1997. "From Peasant Wars to Urban 'Wars': the Antimafia Movement in Palermo." In G. Sider and G. Smith, eds., *Between History and Histories: Making Silences and Commemorations*. Toronto: University of Toronto Press.

Schneider, Peter, Jane Schneider, and Edward Hansen. 1972. "Modernization without Development: the Role of Regional Elites and Non-Corporate

Groups in the European Mediterranean." *Comparative Studies in Society and History* 14: 328–50.

Schor, Ralph. 1985. *L'Opinion française et les étrangers en France 1919–1939*. Paris: Publications de la Sorbonne.

Scidà, Giuseppe. 1990. "Integrazione sociale e pluralismo culturale: prime ipotesi per un'indagine in Sicilia." In M. Colasunto and M. Ambrosini, eds., *Noi e l'altro*. Cesena: Avsi.

Sciortino, Giuseppe. 1988. "Immigrazione extracomunitaria e politiche di blocco." *Segno* 109: 33–48.

    1991. "Immigration into Europe and Public Policy: Do Stops Really Work?" *New Community* 18(1): 89–99.

    1993. "Tra carenza di offerta e 'problema social': atteggiamenti sull'immigrazione degli imprenditori e dei lavoratori della provinca di Bologna." In Marcella delle Donne, Umberto Melotti, and Stefano Petilli, eds., *Immigrazione in Europa*, pp. 425–41. Università degli studi di Roma La Sapienza–Dipartimento di Sociologia. Roma: Centro Europeo di Scienze Sociali (CEDISS).

Sennet, Richard and Jonathon Cobb. 1977. *The Hidden Injuries of Class*. Cambridge: Cambridge University Press.

Senzaconfine. 1989. *Senzaconfine 0*.

Servitium. 1991. *Ero straniero*. Special issue of *Servitium, Quaderni di Spiritualità*, 25(77), Serie Terza.

Sestino, Raffaello. 1989. "La disciplina degli stranieri in Europa." *Democrazia e Diritto* 39(6): 329–53.

Settineri, Daniele and Silvio Governali. 1990. "Intervista a Leoluca Orlando." In Giancarlo Biscardi, Silvio Governali, Rosario Lentini, Enzo Marineo, and Daniele Settinieri, eds., *Trepalermo: società, economia, cultura*, pp. 76–82. Palermo: Edizioni Oida.

SIARES (Società italiana per le analisi e le ricerche economiche e socio-psicologiche). 1988. *Roma: immigrazione dai paesi del Terzo Mondo*. Rome: Ufficio Studi del Comune di Roma.

Silverman, Maxim, ed. 1991. *Race, Discourse and Power in France*. Aldershot: Avebury.

Skellington, Richard, with Paulette Morris. 1992. *"Race" in Britain Today*. London: Sage Publications with the Open University.

Slama, Hassen. 1986. *E la Sicilia scoprì l'immigrazione tunisina*. Palermo: INCA–CGIL Sicilia.

Solomos, John. 1989. *Race and Racism in Contemporary Britain*. London: Macmillan.

Stocking, George W. 1968. *Race, Culture and Evolution*. New York: Free Press.

Sylos Labini, Paolo. 1974. *Saggio sulle classi sociali*. Bari: Laterza.

    1988. "Rapporto fra politica della casa, mobilità, e occupazione." In Liliana Padovani, ed., *Politica o non politica della casa?*, pp. 147–50. Milan: Franco Angeli.

Taguieff, Pierre-André. 1989. "The Doctrine of the National Front in France (1972–1989): a 'Revolutionary' Programme? Ideological Aspects of a National-Populist Mobilization." *New Political Science* 16/17: 29–70.

    1990. "The New Cultural Racism in France." *Telos* 83: 109–22.

Therborn, Göran. 1987. "Migration and Western Europe: the Old World Turning New." *Science* 237: 1183–8.

Van Dijk, Teun A. 1987. *Communicating Racism: Ethnic Prejudice in Thought and Talk.* Beverly Hills, CA: Sage Publications.

1988. "How 'They' Hit the Headlines: Ethnic Minorities in the Press." In G. Smitherman-Donaldson and T. A. Van Dijk, eds., *Discourse and Discrimination*, pp. 221–62. Detroit, MI: Wayne State Press.

1991. *Racism and the Press.* London: Routledge, Chapman & Hall.

Venturini, Alessandra. 1989. "Mercato del lavoro e lavoratori extraeuropei." *Democrazia e Diritto* 34(6): 355–71.

Volpi, Elena. 1990. "Le risposte del COSPE." In Maurizio Bassetti, ed., *Razzismo e immigrazione in Italia.* Special issue of *Testimonianze* 33(3–4): 118–28.

Wallerstein, Immanuel. 1991. "The Ideological Tensions of Capitalism: Universalism versus Racism and Sexism." In Etienne Balibar and Immanuel Wallerstein, *Race, Nation, Class: Ambiguous Identities*, pp. 29–36. New York: Verso.

Wellman, David T. 1993. *Portraits of White Racism.* Second edition. Cambridge: Cambridge University Press.

White, Caroline. 1980. *Patrons and Partisans: a Study of Politics in Two Southern Italian comuni.* Cambridge: Cambridge University Press.

Wieviorka, Michel. 1992. *La France raciste.* Paris: Editions du Seuil.

Wolf, Eric R. 1982. *Europe and the People without History.* Berkeley, CA: University of California Press.

Woods, Dwayne. 1992. "The Crisis of the Italian Party-State and the Rise of the Lombard League." *Telos* 93: 111–26.

Wrench, John and John Solomos, eds. 1993. *Racism and Migration in Western Europe.* Oxford/Providence: Berg.

Zanchetta, Pier Luigi. 1991. *Essere stranieri in Italia.* Milan: Franco Angeli.

Index

Cambridge Studies in Social and Cultural Anthropology

*available in paperback